HOW TO
SURVIVE
IN THE  WILD

Sam Martin and Christian Casucci

Thunder Bay Press

An imprint of Printers Row Publishing Group

10350 Barnes Canyon Road, Suite 100, San Diego, CA 92121

www.thunderbaybooks.com

Conceived and produced by
Elwin Street Limited
3 Percy Street
London W1T 1DE
United Kingdom
www.elwinstreet.com

Printers Row Publishing Group is a division of Readerlink Distribution Services, LLC.

The Thunder Bay Press name and logo are trademarks of Readerlink Distribution Services, LLC.

ISBN: 978-1-62686-666-9

Made in China.

19 18 17 16 15 1 2 3 4 5

HOW TO SURVIVE IN THE WILD

Sam Martin and Christian Casucci

THUNDER BAY
P·R·E·S·S

San Diego, California

Contents

Introduction

Jeff from accounting is leaning over your cubicle wall, droning on about receipts, and all you can hear is the sound of fallen pine needles crunching under your feet. An email arrives from Karen the office manager asking what color highlighters she should order and you reply "campfire," even though you meant yellow. At the water cooler later that day, you imagine yourself in the wild using your paisley tie to lash together a primitive lean-to for refuge from a coming storm.

We all need to retreat into the wilderness once in a while, be it for a weekend escape or the adventure of a lifetime, especially when we're having trouble telling the forest from the trees. But as you sit there amid the safety of your cubicle's three padded walls, you might just wonder if you really have what it takes. Can you survive out there in the great wide open?

In today's world it's not everyone who can hear the call of the wild, much less follow that faint far-off voice that beckons to us from the great outdoors. But for those who do hear it, this is the book for you. Because it's not quite enough just to follow in the direction of that distant call, you've also got to know what to do once you arrive in the vast wilderness. What equipment will you need? How can you protect yourself from the elements? What about finding food and water and keeping warm? And once you're out there, how do you find your way around and eventually get back to civilization when the time comes to return home?

Inside this book you'll find the answers to your many questions, from how to sharpen your knife and properly gut a fish, to how to dig a snow trench or navigate by the stars. Who knows, it may just keep you alive out there. And if all else fails, at least it'll provide you with some nice printed kindling to get your fire going.

CHAPTER 1

Setting out

So you've decided to leave the big city behind and test your mettle in the great outdoors? Thoreau would be proud. Now all you have to do is learn the survival skills, many of which are best gleaned on the trail. Don't just hop in the car with a change of underwear and a sleeping bag; prepare yourself by at least knowing the right gear to bring. And be sure to pack a knife—you can't do anything without a good knife.

The importance of being prepared

Poor preparation for a trip into the great outdoors will dampen even the most enthusiastic expectations. No amount of preparation is too much when you're dealing with Mother Nature, who can be as temperamental and unpredictable as a caged lion. You have to plan what clothes to wear, what and where to eat, and the equipment you'll need to carry it all.

Your knowledge is as important as the gear you bring. In some situations, knowledge can mean the difference between life and death. A first-aid kit is essential. Good ones include materials to treat serious injuries, but the parts you'll use most are bandages, disinfectants, and painkillers. Be sure to bring plenty of these items—you'll be surprised how often you cut, burn, and scrape yourself in the wild.

First-aid kit

✓ Bandages:

　adhesive

　butterfly

　large triangle

✓ Painkillers or analgesics such as acetaminophen or ibuprofen

✓ Antiseptic swabs

✓ Gauze

✓ Athletic tape

✓ Scissors

✓ Needles (for removing splinters and draining blisters)

✓ Moleskin (for blisters)

✓ Rehydration packets (at least two)

✓ Large safety pins

✓ Thermometer

✓ Antidiarrheal pills

✓ Antacid tablets

✓ Two razor blades

✓ Suture equipment

When to go

Part of your preparation is knowing when to go. The most obvious factor is season. If you're looking to do some exploring in the bayous, then maybe August (the peak of hurricane season) isn't the best time to do it. Likewise, for a trip deep into the Rockies in January, snow is not going to make it more fun or more challenging—just more difficult.

There may be seasons that you're not aware of, like the tropical rainy season. As long as you're prepared for a little rain and don't mind it, then this can actually be a great time to visit the equatorial outdoors. Also, don't think that just because you're headed into the desert it's going to be hot all the time. Night under those big cloudless skies encourages the heat to dissipate rapidly, making for cold sleeping weather. Even summers in the desert can have nighttime temperatures as low as 50°F (10°C).

Natural seasons also determine what kind of wildlife might be out and what kind of mood that wildlife might be in. Bears are notoriously aggressive toward the end of the summer and into early fall, when they're trying to fill up on as much food as possible before hibernating for the winter. They're also grumpy when they first wake up in the spring, having gone several months without a meal. Come to think of it, forget seasons when it comes to bears. Just steer clear. In general, winter is a lean time and the animals that are around tend to be more aggressive than during more abundant times of the year. Summers will bring bugs—in some places, lots of them.

Another consideration is human wildlife. If you're really looking to get away from it all, then it's no fun running into a family of four having a picnic while you're trying to fish for your next meal. Savvy trekkers know when peak season is for tourists, and if they'd prefer more solitary experiences, they'll avoid those popular times. Summer holidays, breaks between school terms, and the week between Christmas and New Year are all notoriously busy in most Western countries.

Where to go

If sleeping in your car after losing your house keys late one night is the closest you've come to camping, then maybe going straight to the Yukon for your first destination isn't the best choice.

There are warmer, less rocky places to get started. For that matter, heading deep into the backwoods, deserts, or mountains is always best left to seasoned specialists, especially if those spots are in undeveloped lands like the vast Australian outback, Inner Mongolia, or the Louisiana swamps. More accessible national parks have plenty of wild land to explore and get lost in. The difference is there's usually a park ranger who knows the land like the back of his or her hand and is aware that you're out there somewhere. You should always register with the park before setting out, and let someone know the general direction in which you're headed and for how long. If you haven't reappeared by your expected return date, someone's going to go out looking for you. If you're not in a park, the only things looking for you are the local wildlife—and they will not be offering you a chocolate bar when they find you.

Also, national parks have an infrastructure that can make life in the outdoors more pleasant. Most have full amenities like dedicated tent sites, running water, and bathrooms. They'll also be able to supply information about the flora and fauna you're likely to come across on your daily ramblings—which will help you prepare for your surroundings. National parks also have wild areas without any amenities, for those who want nothing but nature in the raw.

Terrain and climate

All that said, where you should go really depends on what you want to do and feel comfortable with. Not interested in hot sticky weather? Steer clear of the Everglades. Want some high alpine mountaineering and challenging hiking? Try the Rocky Mountains. Desert trekking? Go for Arizona and the Mojave.

It's really up to you how far from or near to civilization you want to be and for how long. As mentioned before, national parks can offer the best of both worlds: nearby ranger stations and camping stores as well as remote locations from which it would take two or three days to walk to the nearest person. If you're just starting to venture into the wilderness it's advisable to first see how you do on a few weekend camping trips to nearby national parks before planning to live in a tent in the forest for eight months. Spending two nights outdoors will give you a good idea of whether you want to spend more or less time under the stars.

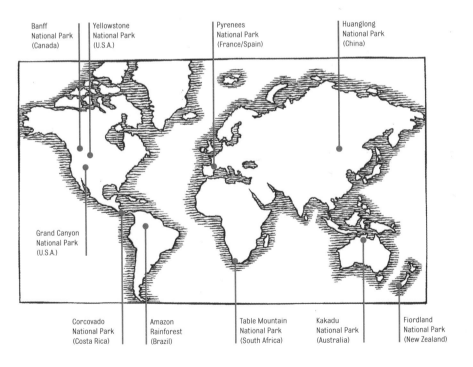

Banff National Park (Canada)

Yellowstone National Park (U.S.A.)

Pyrenees National Park (France/Spain)

Huanglong National Park (China)

Grand Canyon National Park (U.S.A.)

Corcovado National Park (Costa Rica)

Amazon Rainforest (Brazil)

Table Mountain National Park (South Africa)

Kakadu National Park (Australia)

Fiordland National Park (New Zealand)

Basic equipment

One of the best parts about getting out of town is acquiring gear, and there are lots of it to choose from. Just remember that you need to get exactly the things that will keep you warm, sheltered, fed, and healthy—no more and no less.

That means packing light. An extra 5 pounds (2.3 kg) might not sound like much, but it will feel ten times as heavy when you're out on the trail with three hours to go before arriving at the next campsite. Any good outdoor store will list the weight of their gear—everything from tents and sleeping bags to metal camp stoves. Pay attention to this information, and keep a running tally of how much your things weigh. An ounce here or there will add up. Ultralight backpacking enthusiasts boast that their entire kit for summer hiking, without the actual backpack, weighs less than 12 pounds (5.4 kg). Twelve to 20 pounds (5.4–9 kg) is considered lightweight.

In general, start your light-packing strategy by figuring out which tools can do more than one job. A pocketknife with a can opener and corkscrew is an obvious example. Some camp stoves also double as lanterns, though if you have a flashlight you might question the need for a lantern at all. Metal coffee mugs make great soup pans. Also, take a look at the pants that turn into shorts and vice versa with a quick zip just above the knee. You're in the wilderness—who needs fashion?

Small isn't the only thing to consider when you're shopping for lightweight gear. These days, most outdoor gear has a regular option and then a more pricey alternative made with lightweight material. For example, a typical two-person nylon tent might weigh around 5 pounds (2.3 kg), but a tent made with silicone-coated nylon (a much thinner material) can get that weight down to 2 pounds (900 g).

Food is another big weight gain on your load—at least on the way in. We'll take a close look at going light for breakfast, lunch, and dinner in Chapter 5.

Equipment to pack

Carrying equipment

✓ Backpack that's big enough to hold all your gear

✓ Day pack to carry essentials once your camp is set up

Cooking gear

✓ Camping stove and fuel. Many of these stoves accept a variety of fuels.

✓ Cook set that includes a saucepan, frying pan, fork, spoon, and knife

✓ Stainless steel mug

✓ Water bottle

✓ Water purification tablets

✓ Waterproof and windproof matches

✓ Can opener

✓ Fishing kit that includes line, hooks, bobs, and sinkers

Sleeping gear

✓ Sleeping bag, preferably the "mummy" kind that leaves nothing but your eyes, nose, and mouth exposed

✓ Self-expanding sleeping pad

✓ Tent with rain fly (see Chapter 2)

Toiletries

✓ Wash kit for soap, toothbrush, shaving gear, etc.

✓ Insect repellent

✓ Sunscreen

✓ Lip balm

Survival tools

✓ Pocketknife and larger "survival" knife (more on these later)

✓ Head-mounted flashlight—freeing up both hands for other tasks

✓ Sewing kit

✓ Travel candle inside can with lid

✓ Compass, map, and waterproof case

✓ Watch

✓ Whistle

✓ One 20-foot (6-m) length of rope and two 10-foot (3-m) lengths

✓ Wire saw

✓ Sunglasses and binoculars

✓ Toilet paper

Clothes

Spending any amount of time outdoors can be tough on clothes, so always go for quality. Thankfully, the outdoor clothing industry has kept pace with outdoor gear, and you can find lightweight materials that can wick, breathe (and do both at the same time), stretch, insulate, cool, and in one case monitor your heart rate. As a general rule, don't take any more clothing than you can wear at one time.

To know what to bring, first consider the terrain you'll be in. The woods will bring scratchy underbrush and poison ivy—not the most inviting place for walking in shorts. Deserts are hot and dry with very little shade, meaning you'll have to keep yourself cool with thin, billowy materials like linen and provide your own shade in the form of a wide-brimmed hat. Mountains, on the other hand, are rugged and rocky—linen won't last the weekend.

Then there's the issue of bugs. Don't take mosquitoes lightly, especially in tropical regions where dengue fever and malaria can cut a trip painfully short. It might be hot, but take light-colored, long-sleeved cotton shirts and long cotton pants to wear at dusk, when the mosquitoes come out to feed.

There isn't a more important type of gear than the shoes you wear. Rocky, hilly, or mountainous terrain will require hiking boots with good ankle support. But unless you're doing high alpine climbing, there's no need to go overboard. There are some good lightweight leather boots that will work for light and heavy hiking. If you're carrying a light load, you may feel comfortable wearing low-cut trail running shoes. These can work through spring, summer, and fall, and they are less bulky and hot than leather boots. Also important are "camp sandals" for giving your feet a break from the boots. These can be as simple as flip-flops, but we recommend open-toed sandals that strap your foot in at the back. You can wear socks with these if it's chilly, and they're waterproof and very rugged, with well-made soles. Some hikers will set out in their sandals for day hikes or hikes along the beaches and coral outcrops of coasts.

Clothes to pack

Winter

✓ Underwear

✓ Cotton pants that are both thick and lightweight. Be sure you get a pair with nice big pockets on the sides.

✓ Midweight long underwear bottoms

✓ Waterproof rain pants

✓ Long-sleeved cotton T-shirt

✓ Short-sleeved cotton T-shirt

✓ Midweight long underwear top

✓ Midweight fleece jacket

✓ Down-filled coat big enough to fit over your other layers

✓ Outer Gore-Tex rain jacket shell

✓ Several pairs of sock liners

✓ Several pairs of midweight Gore-Tex or wool socks

✓ Boots to fit the terrain you'll be in

✓ Gaiters to keep lower pants dry and protected from thorns

✓ Woolen hat

✓ Mittens, connected by a long string that fits through the sleeves of your jacket

✓ Scarf or neck wrap

✓ Open-toed sandals to wear in camp

Summer

✓ Underwear

✓ Shorts

✓ Pants

✓ Waterproof rain pants

✓ Long-sleeved, light-colored cotton T-shirt (to protect arms from sun and bugs)

✓ Short-sleeved cotton T-shirt

✓ Midweight fleece jacket or sweater

✓ Rain jacket shell

✓ Sock liners

✓ Lightweight socks

✓ Bandana

✓ Wide-brimmed hat or baseball cap

✓ Waterproof open-toed sandals

✓ Lightweight hiking boots

✓ Bathing suit (unless you really want to get back to nature)

Weather forecasting

Unless you're in a place like the Philippines during the rainy season, when you know it's going to rain every day at about three in the afternoon, it might help to be able to get a leg up on the weather by learning a few natural forecasting skills. After all, televisions are hard to come by when you're miles from nowhere.

Cloud language

A quick glance at the clouds can offer a lot of good information about what weather is coming. There are three main types you should know:

Cumulus—Fluffy clouds, generally the ones you can spend hours interpreting as various animals. They usually indicate good weather, but if they're gathered in heaps and suddenly darkening, seek shelter to avoid getting wet.

Stratus—Layered, or spread out, flat clouds. This low-lying cloud can bring rain or snow.

Cirrus—Wispy, resembling curls of hair. These are usually the highest clouds in the sky and generally bring fair weather.

Other clues for predicting the weather

Vegetation, wind, and the sky at night provide clues for predicting the weather:

★ **Plants** before rainfall will usually open up, thereby causing that strong smell in the woods, where it seems like everything is suddenly in bloom.

★ **Prevailing wind shifts** can signal a change in the weather.

★ **A clear sky** at night, as opposed to cloud cover, will generally be colder as there are no clouds to retain heat.

Other methods of forecasting the weather involve watching the animals around you. Cattle, deer, and spiders all have their own way of letting us know that rain is approaching. Cattle will huddle together and face away from the direction that the rain will hit, while deer will head for low ground. Spiders, meanwhile, will cease to spin their webs if they sense that it might rain, making them very valuable companions indeed!

Basic map reading

If you can read a road map, you're ahead of the game when it comes to reading a map where there are no roads. You'll recognize the legend, and you'll also have a handle on scale (or distance) between objects. But there are a few general pointers to picking up a trail map and getting yourself from one hillside to another.

It's comforting to know that all maps around the world use the same set of standards. In general, they show different types of terrain (water, cliffs, vegetation, open spaces, etc.). They also show elevation through the use of contour lines. The closer together these brown squiggly lines are, the steeper the landscape. Having an orienteering map on hand is an essential reference guide for hikers or ramblers who might not be following a premade trail. It can also mean the difference between finding your way home or wandering off a cliff.

Understanding map colors

Map reading starts with knowing what the standard colors on a map mean:

★ **Blue** represents water features from ponds to rivers to oceans.

★ **Black** is given to man-made and rock features such as roads, trails, buildings, cliffs, and boulders.

★ **White** means open woods.

★ **Green** means thick vegetation. Dark green is really thick and usually impassable vegetation.

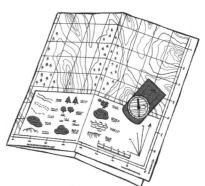

★ **Yellow** is given to open land such as fields.

★ **Brown** is given to features like earth banks or contours.

Cutting and tying

A prepared woodsman should have all the tools and equipment needed to survive in the outdoors. Learning basic skills comes next. The most essential of these basic skills are learning how to use a knife and a length of rope. There's more to it than you think!

Aside from a good pair of boots, there's nothing more essential than a good knife. Use it to cut food or rope. Carve up a sapling for campfire kindling, then fillet a fish for dinner. Knives come in handy in countless ways.

For short-term camping, nothing beats a good pocketknife. You don't have to get the one that has more gadgets than James Bond's, but do get one with more than the corkscrew, which by the way is a must. We've found that a pocketknife with a good blade plus a can opener, bottle opener, scissors, leather awl, fish-carrying hook, screwdriver, toothpick, and tweezers covers the basics. And don't ever knock the toothpick—nothing will take your mind off surviving in the great outdoors like a piece of food stuck between your molars. Getting a knife with a magnifying glass can be a great way to start a fire in a pinch—but avoid the ones with fold-away spoons and forks. They just bulk things up and get things pretty grimy.

If you plan to stay on the wild side a bit longer than a weekend, take the pocketknife but also get a dedicated knife with a good sharp blade that folds in on itself, locks into place when it's out, and has a sturdy handle that fits comfortably in your hand. The blade should be made of high-quality steel and should be about 4 inches (10 cm) long—anything longer tends to be unwieldy and not very useful. This is the one you'll need if you're trapping wild game for food or doing any kind of fishing. The main blades in pocketknives just aren't big or sturdy enough for much more than basic needs. A good survival knife will become your most useful tool and could offer some form of protection against wild animals once all other options have been exhausted. Be sure to get a sturdy leather case that fits on your belt, or a waistband, so that the knife is always where you need it to be: within arm's reach.

Knife skills and safety

Using a knife comes with the obvious care instructions, the first being: *don't cut yourself.* Know this, though: cutting yourself with a dull blade is much worse than cutting yourself with a sharp one. If the blade is nice and sharp, at least the cut will be clean, allowing it to heal faster. A dull blade tends to rip the skin rather than slice it, resulting in uneven cuts that are more difficult to treat. Also, a sharp blade bites into wood, whereas a dull blade slips off more often, which can be dangerous.

Knife-wielding for beginners

★ Whenever you open a knife, be sure the blade locks into place before using it (many knives make a "click" when they lock). If for any reason the blade cannot lock into place, don't use the knife.

★ Fold your knife away after each use.

★ Always carve and cut things with the blade moving away from your body.

★ Never use a knife as a screwdriver or to pry things up—you'll snap off the tip.

★ Always wipe the knife blade after each use. Gunk on the blade will end up in the knife housing and could prevent the locking mechanism from working properly.

★ If you drop your knife while it's open, don't try to catch it; let it fall.

★ Don't run with an open knife.

★ Hand an open knife to someone handle first.

★ Never throw an open knife.

★ Keep knives out of fire. The heat causes the blade to soften.

★ Keep a knife off the ground and away from moisture and dirt.

★ Every four months or so, put a few drops of oil (or some other lubricant) in the locking mechanism of the knife, and wipe a thin layer over the blade itself to prevent it from rusting.

Sharp knife, safe knife

As previously noted, a dull knife is more dangerous and damaging than a sharp knife. Do yourself a favor and spend some time honing your blade.

STEPS

1 If you're using oil, put a few drops of it on the stone and spread it around.

2 For those using water, it's not a bad idea to soak your stone for an hour or two before getting started.

3 Once the stone is prepared, push your knife slowly across the stone at a 20-degree angle, making sure that every part of the blade touches the stone. Don't draw the blade back toward you; instead, push the sharp edge forward.

4 Draw one side of the knife over the stone at least 30 or 40 times. Then repeat the same procedure on the other side.

Using an ax

Investing in a good ax will pay off long after you've moved into your log cabin, especially if you plan on using a wood-burning stove for your winter heat. Even if you live in year-round warmth, an ax in the great outdoors can come in handy for lots of building projects. Like anything you take into the wild, an ax needs to be sturdy and strong enough to last a long time through some tough use. Nothing's worse than breaking an essential tool when you're miles from nowhere.

Whenever you use an ax, don't do it in flip-flops or tennis shoes. Go ahead and put on boots—steel-toed ones preferably. Most ax work is splitting logs for firewood. Get a nice, wide stumplike piece of wood for your cutting block (or if you've got a convenient stump you can use, even better) and put it in an area away from the main living area—you don't want to surprise anyone coming around the side of the log cabin with the blunt end of an ax to the head.

STEPS

1 Place the log you plan to split on the cutting block.

2 With your left hand around the ax handle, near its base, rest the ax head on top of the log you plan to split so that you know how far away to stand from the wood.

3 Stand in front of the log you're going to split on a solid piece of ground with legs apart and squared up to the cutting block.

4 Hold the ax so that your right hand is around the haft just under the ax head, and your left hand is around the base of the haft (or reverse the hands if you're a southpaw).

5 Lift the ax by swinging your left hand forward and pulling the ax back over your right shoulder with your right hand.

6 Bring the ax down onto your target with a natural swing, sliding your right hand down along the haft until it meets your left hand.

Making rope

Making rope isn't for everyone. If you have two days off from work to do some hiking and poking around in the outback, maybe sitting down to weave bark fibers together isn't how you want to spend your time. Then again, what if you get lost on a hike and two days turns into a week in survival mode? Making some rope—or cordage, as it's known in survival circles—might come in handy. It also might help pass the time. Making rope can be surprisingly addictive once you get started.

> **TIP:** The inner bark from linden, elm, hickory, white oak, red or white cedar, mulberry, and chestnut trees is ideal for making rope. The fibrous inner bark of these trees is soft enough to weave but tough enough to create very strong rope. Australian Aboriginals have made rope from baobab trees and the Queensland bottle tree for centuries. The fibrous leaves from the New Zealand flax plant *Phormium tenax* also make for good rope.

STEPS

All you need to make rope is your trusty knife and the inner bark of a tree.

1 When you find the right kind of tree, look for a small green limb protruding from the thicker trunk and cut it off at its base with your knife. Get as many of these green limbs as possible—it takes a lot of bark to make a good strong piece of rope.

2 Take one limb and scrape away the outer bark. The back of a knife (rather than the blade) is the best tool for the job, so that the valuable inner bark doesn't get cut.

3 Once the outer bark is gone, make a cut in the limb along its length, in as straight a line as possible, being careful not to split the limb in two but firm enough to make a clean cut about half an inch (1 cm) deep. Start at the larger base and work your way as far toward the thinner end as possible.

4 Use your thumbs to peel back the inner bark—you should be able to butterfly it open fairly easily. Once you do this for the entire length of the limb, peel the bark completely away from the base and hold it firm. Then flip the limb over and pull the bark free of the limb.

5 Soak the thin piece of bark in a stream or some body of water at least overnight (though some wood may need to be soaked in water to loosen the bark before it comes off the limb). You want the bark to be as soft and pliable as possible.

6 After removing the bark from the water, cut it into strips half an inch (1 cm) thick. A handy way of doing this is to get a big log and stick your knife firmly into it with the sharp blade facing away from you. Then pull the bark slowly toward you so that you're guiding the knife through the bark.

7 When you get about ten strands, hold them evenly in one hand and tie a knot in the top so that all the strands hang down from the knot.

8 Split the strands into two even groups.

9 Twist one group clockwise until it is tight. Tie a knot at its opposite end to keep it from unraveling. Twist the second group of strands until you're left with two tightly twisted pieces of cordage.

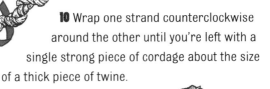

10 Wrap one strand counterclockwise around the other until you're left with a single strong piece of cordage about the size of a thick piece of twine.

11 You can continue to make cordage of this size and tie them end-to-end to get a longer length. If thicker rope is desired, keep wrapping existing rope with other small pieces, but always wrap in the opposite direction from the last wrap. This is called "laying rope."

12 An alternative to laying rope is to braid the strands together. You'll need at least three pieces of twisted-up strands to do this.

Survival knots

Tying knots is one of those things you don't think much about in an office atmosphere, unless you work as an accountant at a rock climbing gym. Get out on the survival trail, however, and you'll find that you need to know at least three different kinds of knots. How else are you going to tie down your tent in a strong wind or lash together ten pieces of wood for a raft? That granny knot just isn't going to cut it anymore. Some terminology you'll need:

Standing end is the stationary end of the rope.
Working end is the one that leads around and through the standing end to make a knot.

Square knot

Also known as a reef knot, a square knot is easy to tie, is very secure, and can be used in a variety of situations. It is mainly used to tie off loose ends. Plus, it's easy to loosen: just push one end toward the knot.

Using two ropes, make an "X" and bring one working end through the loop as if you're tying your shoes. Repeat this process, and you should have the knot. You'll know the knot is done if you can push both ends toward each other.

Bowline

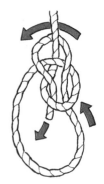

Some people call this the "king of knots." It should be called the rescue knot. If it's done right, it forms a quick, nonslipping loop—perfect for tying around people you're trying to haul off the mountain. Climbers use it a lot.

Begin by making a loop in the standing end of the rope. Then take the working end up through the loop around the standing part and back in the direction it came from.

Clove hitch

The best lashing knot is the clove hitch. It's easy on the rope, and because the rope crosses over on itself, the knot actually gets stronger the more pressure is exerted on it.

Loop the rope over the timber. Pass the working end over and across itself and around the timber again. Then take the working end and feed it under itself so that it comes out in the opposite direction to the standing end.

Timber hitch

When you're building your log cabin, there will be a lot of dragging of logs from the forest to your site. For this, the only knot you need to know is the timber hitch.

Loop your rope around a log and bring the working end up and around the standing end of the rope. Bring the working end back down the way you came, and bring it over and under itself two or three times. When the standing end is pulled, the knot tightens onto itself.

Sheet bend

In some situations you need to tie the end of a small rope to the end of a large rope. This is the knot. It's called a sheet bend because sailors used it to "bend the sheets" or tie the ropes in the rigging of a ship. This could come in handy if you're stranded on a deserted island and are planning an escape by raft and homemade sail.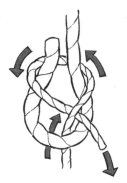

Form a loop with the larger rope. Thread the smaller rope through the loop and bring the working end around the larger rope's loop. Bring the small rope back under itself, but don't go back through the loop. Pull tight.

Securing and building

Knowing good knife safety or the usefulness of a few good knots for a weekend away is one thing, but for those longer stays in the great outdoors, you will need to learn advanced skills.

Lashing techniques

The longer you're in the wild, the more you'll find to do. In fact, the more you'll want to do to keep yourself from going crazy with boredom. When you start digging in more permanently, there are some techniques you'll need to know, such as lashing. Whether you're building a fire screen, a raft, or a primitive sled, being able to tie small logs together with the rope you make can really save the day. Many of the building and survival projects covered later in the book use these lashing techniques, so pay attention.

Lashing is an excellent way to hold pieces of timber together when nails are in short supply. You can make semipermanent shelters, rafts, tables, chairs, gurneys, and other equipment with this construction technique. There are two different kinds of lashing techniques you can employ if you're tying timbers together at right angles to one another. They are called "square lashing" and "diagonal lashing."

HOW TO SQUARE LASH

1 First tie a clove hitch on one timber right where the crosspiece will go.

2 When you put the crosspiece in place, take the working end of the rope and loop it over the crosspiece, under the first piece, over the crosspiece again, and back under the first piece. Do this three or four times.

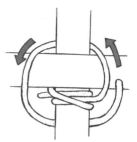

3 After that's done, loop the working end of the rope back over the first piece and under the crosspiece.

4 Tie it off with a clove hitch on the same timber you tied the first clove hitch to, only do this one on the other side of the crosspiece.

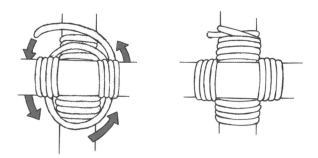

HOW TO DIAGONAL LASH

1 Tie a clove hitch to one timber.

2 Wrap the rope around both timbers in a diagonal fashion three times. Make sure the rope-turns lie next to each other, not on top of each other.

3 Wrap the rope around both timbers in the opposite diagonal direction. Pull them tight.

4 Loop the working end around both timbers, going over one and under the other.

5 Tie it off with a clove hitch on the same timber you tied the first one to, only on the opposite side of the crosspiece.

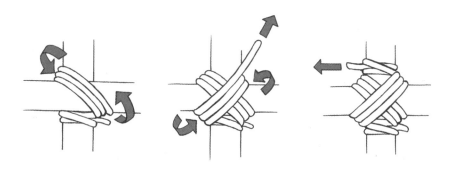

Sewing

Even while you're considering the possibilities of a large log cabin, you still have to take care of the small stuff. Holes in your clothes will invite unwanted bugs and weather into your inner world, as will a rip in the tent. If you're on a deserted island and you're planning on sailing out of there as soon as you lash together some timbers for a boat, don't forget that you packed a sewing kit—so you can make a sail.

If you know you're going to be in the wild for a while, beef up that kit with a few extra needles, such as a large sailmaker's needle, a packing needle, and a curved needle. You'll also need to know a few different types of strong stitches.

Straight stitch

This is the most basic stitch. It's good for patches on your jeans or other lightweight material but not much more. You put the needle through the patch and the pants, then come back up a few millimeters in front of it before going back down a few millimeters in front of that. The stitch looks like a dotted line.

TIP: Your sewing is only as strong as your thread. Fishing line makes for a very sturdy seam, if you're not bothered about looks. Or you can double up your thread for extra strength.

Crossover stitch

Crossover stitches are used to join two seams together, among other things. It's more sturdy than the straight stitch, and it's very simple to master. The needle works in the same way as the straight stitch but in a side-to-side diagonal manner.

Cross-stitch

The cross-stitch is a sturdy stitch that has great holding strength. It can be used on most materials, including leather and sail materials. It is accomplished by sewing a crossover stitch and then coming back down, crossing over the original thread.

Blanket stitch

The toughest and most secure stitch is the blanket stitch. Each stitch essentially locks in on itself with a semiknot. That means the seam or stitch can only come apart one stitch at a time. The blanket stitch is worked from left to right. The needle is brought up vertically and brought out of the fabric with the thread tucked under the needle.

CHAPTER 2

Shelter

Anyone who has ever been stranded in the wilderness with little more than their wits to see them through knows that shelter is one of the top four priorities for survival (the other three are first aid, food, and water). Luckily, if you didn't come prepared with a shelter, such as a tent, you can construct one yourself. You'll find that with a few simple tools, the materials you find around you, and some perseverance, a variety of shelters—from simple to elaborate—can soon be giving you cover.

Give me shelter

For anybody living out in the wilderness, spending the night in the great outdoors is one of the thrills of the adventure. Shelters represent a safe haven and a home away from home.

Practically speaking, shelters provide respite from inclement weather—a place to get in from the rain, sleet, snow, and wind. In the coldest parts of the world during the winter, getting out of the weather is absolutely essential. Without a shelter, the exposure to wind and snow can bring on hypothermia quickly when you're not on the move.

Shelters become the centerpiece for your wilderness camp, the thing around which everything else revolves. Your shelter is your headquarters from which all adventure is organized and initiated. When times get tough, knowing that you have this home base can provide a jolt of confidence for any weary soul.

What kind of shelter you build depends on the season, unless you have a good three- or four-season tent that can withstand most of what Mother Nature throws at you. During the spring, weather comes in all varieties. It can be cold, icy, and wet—sometimes very wet. If you're not using a tent, you'll have to make sure that whatever you do use is watertight. Summer may be the best time of year to sleep outdoors. Springtime shelters work well during these months, as long as you make sure there's enough of a breeze coming in to ease the heat. But in summer, there's always the possibility of sleeping au naturel—out under the stars like a true bushman. It's a thrill, and there's nothing like waking up on a bed of pine needles with the sun peeking over the eastern horizon. Then again, there's nothing like waking up with dozens of mosquito bites on your face and neck, either. Plan accordingly. When you get into fall and early winter, shelters need to be well insulated and paired with a campfire, usually located just outside your shelter's entrance.

Deep winter shelters are another matter altogether, and they usually consist of ice caves and igloos—neither of which you really want to end up in unless it's an emergency.

Setting up camp

Most wilderness lovers will be erecting or using temporary shelters—as opposed to a limestone and log cabin with a walk-out basement and a mailbox. One of the first things to be done after arriving at a wilderness destination is to choose the best spot to pitch a tent (or throw up a lean-to). None are perfect, so do the best you can.

★ The site should be flat and smooth. If possible, try to locate previously used campsites.

★ The site should be in a raised location so that rain won't pool around the shelter.

★ Don't choose a site closer than 80 yards (75 m) to a river or stream. Sudden rains can make them swell.

★ Don't camp right next to outdoor toilets. Aside from the obvious smelly reasons, the foot traffic and lights will be a disturbance.

★ Avoid sites under trees with lots of dead branches in them.

★ Avoid getting pounded by rockslides by steering clear of sites next to or right under rocky slopes.

★ In summer, choose a spot that will be shaded most parts of the day but especially in the afternoon when the sun is hottest.

★ In winter, choose a site that's exposed to the sun and on higher ground (cold air collects in depressions in the ground).

★ If there are lots of mosquitoes or blackflies out, find a spot in the prevailing wind. Mosquitoes hate wind.

Locating the perfect campsite

The first step to setting up camp is finding the perfect campsite. Word to the wise: always get to where you're going well before nightfall. Not only is it going to be hard setting up camp in total darkness, but it'll be nearly impossible to pick a good site in the first place.

With plenty of daylight left after finding your perfect site, decide where your tent (or other temporary shelter) is going to go. If there are trees, put it there. Trees are great for providing much-needed shade during the summer and protection from the elements the whole year. If you're setting up your kitchen area underneath hanging branches, then you do need to beware of the drips and falling debris that accompany downpours. If you cannot locate any natural shade, then you can create your own using branches or a spare tarp, if you have one handy.

Locate your campfire away from any low-hanging branches. Next, begin clearing the land where you plan to sleep of rocks, twigs, and pinecones. There's no need to excavate and grade the location with a bulldozer; just sweep any fallen debris away with your hands and feet. Protruding stumps or rocks might mean that you need to find another site.

Tents, of course, are the most common types of temporary shelters, though if you find yourself without a tent for one reason or another (let's say an ember from last night's campfire turned your tent into ash), then you might want to know about some alternatives. Lean-tos, Navajo hogans, debris shelters, and snow caves are all available to the resourceful. These temporary shelters can be made with minimum skill from materials found in nature.

HOW TO SET UP CAMP

1 Pitch your tent or build your temporary shelter.

2 Roll out your sleeping bag inside the shelter.

3 Collect any dead branches you find around your site and stack them next to the fire pit. If there is no fire pit, make one (see Chapter 4).

4 Set up a camp chair, or roll a log into place, next to the fire pit.

5 Light the fire.

6 When the fire is going, get out your cookware and that night's supper. Any food you don't intend to use should come out of your pack and tent and be placed in a secure spot on the other side of the campsite. If you have the means, you can suspend food from a low tree branch with a rope and bag. This prevents wild animals from rooting through your stuff—and you from looking for a midnight snack!

Tents

Since tents are the most common form of shelter one can lug into the wilderness, it helps to know a bit about them. A quick foray into any outdoor store will reveal an overwhelming selection of tents, from the one-person bivy bag to the three-room family fun house.

Choosing a tent depends on how large an interior you need, how much weight you want to carry, and how much money you have to spend. You can find out how big a tent is on the inside by visiting an outdoor store—most have the tents already set up. Make sure what you're buying is going to be big enough. If you know you'll be adventuring with a partner, don't try to save money by getting a one-person tent. There will be no restful sleeps if you do.

The tent you need depends on your outdoor experience. If you're just hitting a state park for a few summer weekends, then don't buy an expensive four-season mountaineering setup. If you might try more than just summer camping in the next couple of years, consider a three-season tent that can be opened up for hot weather and covered for rain and moderately cold weather. Extreme cold requires expedition tents made with heavier materials and waterproof floors that extend part of the way up the tent walls.

In general, the signs of a good-quality tent are thick, sturdy tent poles; double-sewn seams (poor seams are most likely to cause leakages, which will leave you wet and unhappy!); and heavy-duty zippers on the doors. Also, if your tent does not have twin layers, then it's probably a good idea to invest in one that does. Two layers allow for insulation if it rains, which means that there will be a gap between the external—and wet—layer and the inside layer closest to you.

A good rain fly is a must too. These should come all the way to the ground and have a means of adjustment so they have good tension. Also, three- and four-season tents often come with vestibules—small "rooms" just off the front door (expedition tents usually have two vestibules). These have their own zippered door and allow you to get in out of the rain to take your boots and wet clothes off before going into the tent proper—a very helpful addition if you think you'll be in the rain for any extended period of time.

TIP: Keep it legal. No matter what kind of shelter you decide to pitch or build, make sure you're aware of local permissions or building codes. Not every national park lets you interrupt the natural flora to piece together a lean-to or a Navajo hogan. Sometimes they provide crude shelters for you, which normally require that you book ahead to reserve the space. Most of the time, parks have cleared campsites for the tent camper. If you aren't in a national or state park but on wild land, there are still rules to abide by when it comes to erecting most kinds of shelters. And clearly it's illegal to set up shop on private land, though you can always try requesting permission from the owner. Even if you buy a piece of land with the intention of building a log cabin and living far out in the wilderness, there are building codes, property line setbacks, sewage considerations, and other standards to consider. Usually, local town or city governments can provide you with the necessary information to make sure you build within the bounds of the law.

Making your own shelter

There are a number of shelters you can build from materials found in nature. If you happen to find yourself without a tent, or if you just want to go a little more rustic, these are good shelter solutions. In winter, snow caves or snow trenches can keep you warm in dire situations, but they probably aren't the first choice for most adventurers.

Lean-to

A lean-to is a "wall" of natural materials leaned up against a tree or stone. All you need are some wrist-sized pieces of wood and some boughs or branches. Simply make a large rectangle and fill in the area with wood lashed together. Lay the structure against a tree or rock, and cover the outside with branches or boughs. It might be helpful to weave the branches into the sticks below.

Debris shelter

Similar to a lean-to but more sturdy and less temporary, a debris shelter is like a personal cave made out of sticks, mud, leaves, and branches. A tripodlike combination of poles or sticks is used to hold up the walls. The main pole is the ridge pole, which forms the backbone of the shelter. It's held up by two side sticks and extends down to the ground. Once the tripod is in place, line the ridge pole with more sticks. After this, thatch the whole thing in mud, leaves, branches, and brush. A well-built debris shelter can keep out strong rains and wind.

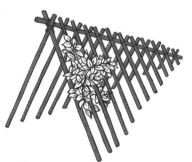

Snow trench

In extremely cold conditions, it's important to get out of the elements, and if there's lots of snow around, you'll have plenty of material to build with. Think igloo. Snow may be cold to the touch, but it has insulating qualities that can keep a person much warmer than if they were exposed to a north wind. A snow trench is part trench and part igloo. Just cut blocks of snow out of a long, 3-foot (90-cm) wide trench, and use the blocks to build walls and a flat roof over the trench. When it's done, you'll at least have a place to lie down.

Tree-pit snow shelter

Another benefit of snow is that it can get deep. For those looking for shelter, this is a good thing. A tree-pit snow shelter is made by digging snow out around a tree to make a pit. The top of the pit is covered by leaning branches onto the tree trunk in a teepeelike formation. A person can curl around the tree at the bottom of the pit for warmth.

TIP: Temperatures should reach at least the freezing point in order for your snow trench shelter to be effective—otherwise you may find your shelter melting on you.

Building a cabin

If you've been spending lots of time outdoors, living in temporary shelters here and there can get a little, well, exhausting. Snow caves, for example, won't bring much joy past the beginning of spring. Building a log cabin, on the other hand, is a way to put down solid roots and carve out your wilderness Shangri La once and for all.

Of course, home construction—however primitive—isn't for everyone, and the guidelines spelled out below are just that: guidelines. Anyone serious about building a log cabin should consult with a professional builder and consider buying a set of plans. Likewise, knowledge of any local building codes is essential. Also, this is the kind of job that cannot be done without the right tools and materials—we list the essentials below, but if you've never used a chainsaw, think seriously about getting a lesson from someone who has.

Selecting a site for your cabin

Next to solid construction techniques, site selection is the single most important part of building a cabin in the wilderness. The site will affect interior heating and cooling, accessibility, and views. It will also determine how dry you stay during the rainy seasons. It may sound obvious, but here it is anyway: don't build on floodplains. In general, a site should have good drainage (i.e., water drains away from it without any help from you), so that the foundation doesn't sit in water. Water is the number-one enemy of any wood building, and much of what you do during the planning and building process involves finding ways to keep it out of, off of, and away from your structure.

Selecting a site will in large part depend on the climate of where you're building. Those in colder climates will want the longest side of their cabin to be the south-facing side (or north-facing in the southern hemisphere), with unobstructed access to the sun. In the winter, the sun will heat up walls and shine in windows to provide a free source of heat. Conversely, in warmer climates, one should minimize this side of the house. Large roof overhangs on this side are a good idea in any climate, because they'll provide shade from the summer sun (the sun rises much higher during summer months), while letting in the lower winter sun.

There is also the issue of terrain. Don't choose a site that's so remote and difficult to reach that you have to helicopter all your materials in. That gets expensive. Also, don't build in low-lying areas: cold air gathers in depressions. In the building industry, these are called "frost pockets" because they're the first places to freeze. Water gathers in low-lying areas as well. For several reasons, a sloped site can actually be a benefit to cabin building. Water will drain naturally. If the site is very sloped, you can build into the side of it to help insulate in winter and keep the house cool in summer. This kind of building can also help keep strong winds from blowing directly onto the house. To build into the side of a slope, you will need heavy equipment to dig out the earth. That's an extreme case, and most of the time a more level site is best. You'll have to adjust the foundation footings to get an exact base no matter what.

Lastly, choose a site that's close to the trees you're going to cut down and build with. There's no sense in making the job harder than it already is.

TIP: If you'd like a little help, log home kits can be purchased. These include timber logs sized to your specifications and delivered straight to your selected site.

Planning

It's not essential, but it helps to know the basic measurements of your log cabin before you choose a site. That way you can make the site fit to your cabin plans rather than vice versa. This is especially true for complex designs; but for the following example we're going to build a one-room 14 x 14-foot (4.2 x 4.2-m) log cabin with 8-foot (2.4-m) walls and a sloping shed roof— a compact building that can fit almost anywhere, so planning for site selection is no problem.

HOW TO PLAN YOUR CABIN

1 Draw the basic floor plan of the cabin, including exterior walls and door and window openings.

2 Mark and write in all measurements for wall lengths as well as door and window openings. Windows can vary in size, so make sure you determine exactly which windows you will use and find out the width and height of each one before drawing your plans. Door sizes are more common. All of them are usually 80 inches (2 m) high. Widths can be 30, 32, and 36 inches (76, 80 and 90 cm). Again, pinpoint a door you'll use and make your plans according to its specific size.

3 Determine measurements from the corner of the cabin to any window or door openings. Mark and write in these measurements on the plan. Be sure to determine measurements between windows and between windows and doors.

4 Draw a rough sketch of all four sides of the cabin in elevation, taking into account the sloping roof. A shed roof slopes downward from front to back. The easiest way to plan for the roof is to add a foot onto the front wall to bring its measurement up to 9 feet (2.7 m). That gives you a slope of 3:4, or 3 inches every 4 inches (or 3 cm every 4 cm)—a very slight pitch but one that will certainly keep the rain off. For those building in areas likely to get heavy snows, consider adding at least another foot (30 cm) onto the front wall to get a steeper roof pitch to encourage the snow to slide off easier.

Tools

As you might imagine, building a log cabin requires a lot of woodworking tools, and it's possible to go nuts at your local home improvement center with all the choice. Portable saw mills, wood lathes, power drill presses, and every other kind of tabletop power tool could easily be put to good use. As could a good chainsaw. They are, however, not altogether necessary—or practical—especially when you have no access to electricity. Given the choice from the above list, a gas-powered chainsaw would be the cabin-builder's first choice. But alas, chainsaws aren't always practical, either. For one thing, gasoline may not always be readily available. Here's a list of essentials:

Essential tools

- ✓ Ax
- ✓ Sharpening stone
- ✓ Hammer
- ✓ Assorted nails
- ✓ Hand saws
- ✓ Drill
- ✓ Tape measures
- ✓ Carpenter's square
- ✓ Shovel
- ✓ Spirit level
- ✓ Plumb line
- ✓ Large wood chisel and wood mallet
- ✓ A large draw knife to remove bark from logs

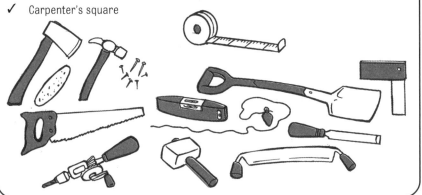

Selecting timber

Gathering materials for your log cabin means first and foremost getting some logs. That means cutting down a few trees that are between 8 and 12 inches (20–30 cm) in diameter and about 30 feet (9 m) tall. Felling trees this size is hard and dangerous work and not for beginners. If possible, get help from an experienced woodsman and use every precaution while you're out there, including ear and eye protection and steel-toed boots.

Pine is one of the best types of tree to build with, while hardwood trees like poplar or willow are not recommended. Also, because the moisture content in wood causes it to expand and shrink during wet and dry times of the year, it's essential to season your logs for at least six months before you build with them. This dries out the wood sufficiently so that you won't have problems with the logs expanding or shrinking out of level during the building process. Choose a tree that's straight and isn't in a very dense part of the forest. The tree needs to have space to fall all the way to the ground once you cut it and not get caught up in other trees' branches or in any vines.

Felling timber

Chopping down a tree is not as easy as cutting into one side until the tree falls over. There are specific steps to follow so that you don't get hurt and so that your tree doesn't fall on the neighbor's camper.

STEPS

A chainsaw (or ax) as well as a bondsaw are essential in order to successfully chop down a tree.

1 Take a close look at the lay of the tree to determine if it's leaning one way or the other. The tree will naturally want to fall in the direction it's already leaning.

2 If there is no obvious lean to the tree, choose the direction in which you want the tree to fall—known in tree-cutting circles as the "felling path."

3 Cut a notch in the tree on the side of the felling path. The notch should be about a foot off the ground. The size of the notch will depend on the diameter of the tree, but in general it should be at a 15- or 20-degree angle, 6 inches (15 cm) tall on the face and about 3 inches (7.5 cm) deep at the bottom. Standing to the side of the tree, make the downward angle cut first. Then make a horizontal cut to meet the first cut. Remove the wedge of wood you've just cut out.

4 Now go around to the back of the tree and mentally determine your escape routes. When the tree starts to come down, you'll want to use them. Plan to walk quickly and surely at a 45-degree angle back from the tree to a spot at least 10 feet (3 m) away as the trunk comes down. Most felling accidents happen when a falling tree kicks back or slides off to the side of the stump as it's coming down.

5 Once your escape route is planned, make the back cut. Saw through the back of the trunk toward the notch you cut earlier. Make sure your cut will meet up with the horizontal cut of the notch and not through the notch face. Cut to within about an inch (2.5 cm) of the notch. The tree should start to topple at this point.

6 As soon as you see the tree move toward its felling path, turn around and walk quickly along your escape route.

Transporting timber to your site

Once the tree is down, you now have to get it to the building site. This is when you'll be glad you selected a site close to the log supply.

Before moving the log, you first have to limb and top it. That means cutting off all limbs as well as the top of the tree, which is usually thinner than the usable trunk. Since we're going to be building a 14 x 14-foot (4.2 x 4.2-m) cabin, it wouldn't hurt to go ahead and saw the trunk into 14-foot (4.2-m) lengths—a process known as "bucking." Doing all this at the felling site, rather than back at the building location, makes for less mess around the new cabin and a much easier transportation job.

In years past, dragging or skidding freshly felled tree trunks out of the forest was done with a horse or a tractor and some strong rope. Trunks were then loaded onto trucks or put in rivers for a "log drive." Some lumberjacks used a method of transportation called "timber rafting," in which they lashed logs together into a raftlike mass before sending them downstream. This prevented logjams—common on log drives—and kept all your trees together. During log drives it was common for several logging companies to toss their logs into the river along with everyone else. They would "brand" the logs before doing it so they could pick them out of the pack, but it was time-consuming work.

If you don't have a horse or a tractor, then getting your logs back to camp is going to take some good old hard work. Simply tie a rope around one end of the trunk and start pulling. It might help to use a towel or other form of padding around the rope at your end so that you can loop it over your shoulder without the rope cutting into your skin.

TIP: Now it's time to get building. If you haven't already enlisted some friends to help, do so. With four of you working together, this cabin could be ready to move into within a month.

The building process
Stage one: the foundation

1 Measure out the walls with a tape measure. Leave about 1 foot (30 cm) of space on all sides, making a slightly smaller square inside the area of the eventual cabin. Place rocks at the four corners.

2 Set up batter boards (horizontal boards nailed to posts) 2 feet (60 cm) from each corner and at the halfway point between the corners on all four sides.

3 Tie string between the batter boards to create a string grid. Where strings cross is the location of a foundation footing. There should be nine in total— one at each corner, one at each halfway mark, and one in the middle.

4 Check that all the measurements are exact; retie string if necessary.

5 Dig holes 2 feet (60 cm) deep at each string intersection.

6 Fill holes with medium-sized rocks, making sure to mix in earth as you do.

7 Level out the string grid. Where strings intersect, make sure they are touching. This ensures that the floor of your cabin isn't going to be sloped.

8 Stack two flat rocks on top of each other at the location of each foundation footing. The rocks should just touch the string grid at each location. If necessary, remove or add any medium-sized rocks and earth to get an exact level for each footing.

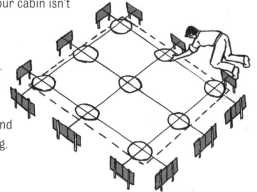

Stage two: the floor

YOU WILL NEED

✓ Three large 14-foot (4.2-m) logs

✓ Eight very straight medium-sized 12-foot (3.6-m) logs

✓ Five sheets of plywood, each 4 x 8 feet (1.2 x 2.4 m)

✓ Ax

✓ Hand saw

---

1 Lift each large 14-foot (4.2-m) log onto the foundation footings so that each one spans three footings. These are the floor sills. Place them parallel with the front of the house. Since the foundation footings measure 12 feet (3.6 m) between corners, be sure to allow the 14-foot (4.2-m) sills to overhang equally on each side of the foundation.

2 Place the medium-sized logs on top of the floor sills. These are your floor joists. Each one will run perpendicular to the floor sills, and they will be spaced 18 inches (45 cm) from each other. Start laying floor joists 1 foot (30 cm) from the end of each sill to account for the 14-foot (4.2-m) sill lengths (your interior floor area will be exactly 12 x 12 feet [3.6 x 3.6 m]).

3 To prevent the joists from rolling off the floor sills, notch the ends and the middle of each log so that it fits snug on top of the sills.

4 Once all the floor joists are in place, nail down plywood on top of them. You should be able to fit four full 4 x 8-foot (1.2 x 2.4-m) sheets in place before having to cut the last one in half to measure 4 x 4 feet (1.2 x 1.2 m).

Stage three: the walls

1 Use an ax and saw to notch out two logs to fit on top of the floor-sill extensions at both ends of the floor.

2 Notch out two more logs so they will fit over the two logs you just placed, being sure to fit the log snug against the floor joists. The notches will lock the corners of the walls in place, so there's no need to use nails here.

3 Repeat the above steps, notching and stacking logs up to a height of 8 feet (2.4 m). Make the notches deep enough so that each log locks over the previously laid log and rests on top of the log below it. Don't worry about gaps between the logs.

4 For the wall where the front door will be, cut the logs to fit on either side of the door before notching one end to make the front corners. Toenail the logs together where they rest on top of each other at the door opening. Toenailing is securing two boards together by driving nails at an angle through one and into the other. In this case, if two logs are laying on top of each other, instead of hammering a nail through the top of one and into the other, nail at an angle through the end of one log and down into the top of the log below. They'll be further secured with the door frame.

5 As with the front door, be sure to account for any windows in the cabin.

6 To account for the shed roof, add one more log onto the top of the front wall. This header log should be at least twice as thick as the logs below it. This will give the roof the slope it needs to shed rainwater and snow.

Stage four: windows and doors

YOU WILL NEED

✓ Prehung windows and doors

✓ Hammer

✓ Nails

1 Fit windows and doors into rough openings and nail the frames to the log ends.

2 Again, don't worry about gaps in between the window and door frames—they will get filled later.

Stage five: roof

YOU WILL NEED

✓ Seven medium-sized logs, each 16 feet (4.8 m) long

✓ Eight sheets of plywood, each 4 x 8 feet (1.2 x 2.4 m)

✓ Metal roofing material (corrugated iron or tin)

✓ Roofing screws

✓ Electric screw gun or screwdriver

1 Notch all seven logs to fit over the logs at the top of the front and back walls. Allow for 1-foot (30-cm) overhangs on each side. These are the roof joists.

2 Nail down the plywood to the roof joists. The roof area will be 16 x 16, or 256 square feet (4.8 x 4.8 m or 23.04 m²). You should be able to fit all eight pieces of plywood onto the roof joists without having to cut any of them.

3 Once the plywood is in place, screw down the metal roofing. To prevent roof leaks, be sure to get 16-foot (4.8-m) lengths of corrugated metal or standing-seam roofing material.

4 Screw down the metal roofing into the peaks of the corrugated metal or into the tops of the standing seams. If you screw into the valleys where the water runs, you'll be inviting leaks.

5 Overlap each roofing section to the next to hide seams.

6 Build out the side walls of the cabin from the walls up to the roof. Saw or cut logs at an angle to match the angle of the roof. Notch logs to the front corner and toenail logs to each other toward the back to secure them. Once the roof is on, there will be triangle-shaped gaps between the side walls of the cabin and the sloping roof above. To fill in these gaps, stack and secure logs to the top of each side wall by notching the logs at the front corner and toenailing the logs toward the back. These logs will also need to be cut at an angle to match the angle of the sloping roof.

Stage six: chinking

YOU WILL NEED

✓ A mixture of mud and straw   ✓ Putty knife

1 Fill gaps between logs and between door and window frames with a mixture of mud and straw. Dig down deep to get mud with a good clay content.

2 For large gaps, fill with strips of wood, then roll mud and straw into balls and push the mixture into the gaps over any added wood.

3 Use a putty knife to smooth out the chinking.

4 Leave to dry for two full days.

Long term: hearth and home

As your survival training gets better and you graduate slowly from a lean-to to a permanent dwelling, you won't want to have to withstand the elements to get to your campfire. It's time to get that fire indoors.

Freestanding stoves

Perhaps the easiest to come by and arguably the most romantic form of indoor fireplace is the good old pot-bellied stove—known more often in these modern times as a freestanding stove. A hundred years ago, there wasn't a log cabin in all of Canada without a freestanding wood-burning stove and a stovepipe poking up through the roof. Smoke billowing from these iron chimneys was a sure sign that Trapper John was home from the hunt, most likely with a pot of coffee and a slab of salmon cooking on top of his cast-iron heater.

These days, wood isn't the only thing burning. That's because burning wood gives off notoriously high levels of carbon monoxide and other gases—none of them good for your health. So the industry has come up with gas, electric, and coal stoves. They look the same but use different fuels. That said, wood stoves still have the highest heating efficiency of them all. Because of this, the pot-bellied industry has gone to great lengths to clean them up, outfitting stoves with all kinds of air flow and clean-burning technologies (in the United States, wood-burning stoves must meet government standards before they hit the market). One highly efficient form of wood-burning stove is the pellet stove. These burn handfuls of tiny pellets made from sawdust that are automatically fed into the burner; not only are they efficient but they're also much cleaner.

If you want one, you'll find dozens of different styles to choose from. Handsome cast-iron dinosaurs can be found in antique stores, though these do emit a lot of carbon monoxide, so be sure to leave a window cracked if you go this route and never leave a fire going overnight.

New cast-iron models have glass doors and are often clad in brightly colored porcelain or other types of radiant stone, like soapstone. This absorbs the heat from the flame and radiates it out into the room. Some new models even come with accessories like drying racks for wet gloves and socks, or stove-top steamers to humidify the air during the dry depths of winter.

HOW TO SET UP A WOOD-BURNING STOVE

Getting the campfire out of the cold woods and into a freestanding stove doesn't mean you should leave behind the safety tips. Check local building codes to ensure proper setup. For general advice, here are some things to consider:

1 All freestanding stoves, regardless of fuel type, need to be placed on a fireproof floor. Tile, concrete, and brick all work fine. Stone slabs, preferably soapstone or firebrick—something that can absorb and radiate heat effectively—have a perfectly rustic look.

2 Cabin walls surrounding a stove—unless of course the stove is in the middle of the room—need to be clad in some kind of fireproof material such as metal, cement board, or brick.

3 Keep as much of the chimney inside the house as possible to retain heat.

4 Chimneys should extend above the highest point of the cabin roof.

5 Now that the fire is inside, make sure you have enough firewood there, too. Always leave room for a stack of fuel near the stove.

CHAPTER 3

Water

Water, that colorless, transparent, and odorless liquid that fills the bodies of our seas, lakes, and rivers, is also what fills up the majority the human body—75 percent of it, to be exact. This vital liquid performs so much work in keeping our bodies going that to be without it for even a few days could spell disaster, and not just because of how bad you'll smell after a few days without a shower.

The thirsty body

One good thing about fat is that it aids in storing food in our bodies, but as far as water goes, we have no such inner storage system. We're always losing water, whether through bathroom breaks or perspiration, and we need to constantly replenish what we've lost.

When out and about in nature, the need for water far outweighs the need for food, so finding and gathering this essential liquid should always take precedence over hunting for your next meal. A week or more without food in the wilderness, while not anybody's idea of a great time, is manageable. But a few days without water, even less time when out in the desert, can be costly, because the body will immediately start to undergo an inevitable breakdown.

Water consumption, depending on region and climate, will vary. In general, anywhere from 6–10 pints (3.5–5.5 liters) a day should suffice for the average person. But keep in mind that in a hotter locale like Death Valley, the average human body will require more water than one that's in a more temperate area. High levels of activity may also require you to raise your water intake. In any region, no matter how pure the source of water seems to be, purifying your water first is a must, as one can never tell what contaminants and harmful organisms might be present.

Put simply, water equals life. It's no secret why many ancient civilizations built their great cities on the banks of mighty rivers or on the shores of a great ocean, so do as your forebears once did and make water your number-one priority. Once procured, never take it for granted but instead treat it like the vital gift it is.

Like the rest of us, water obeys the laws of gravity. When snow falls on a mountaintop and melts with the coming spring, it only has one place to go: straight down to the base of the mountain. This is where you'll find a freshwater spring or a raging river to slake your thirst.

The gravity factor is not just for the mountains, as the same approach works in more arid locales as well. In a sandy environment like the desert,

look for the low points in the ground between dunes. In flatter areas, search for bowl-shaped depressions with smooth sides. Both of these can indicate where water may have accumulated and pooled during rain. Once you've located your spot, just dig down a few feet in the sand until it becomes wet, then a little deeper until water seeps into your hole.

Temporary water sources

Coming across a glistening and flowing stream when your water bottle is down to its last few swallows is like a gift from the heavens, but what if you haven't seen a body of water for days and you're not sure when you will? Water comes from many sources—it doesn't always have to be a rushing river that quenches your thirst.

Rainfall

It is not often that rain is welcomed by wood-dwellers, but if you've tapped out all of your other water sources and you're desperately in need of a serious drink, you may find yourself doing a rain dance to encourage the downpour. By simply placing enough containers around your site to catch what falls, you can have rainwater account for a substantial amount of your drinking water. One of the simplest methods of collection is to angle your tent top toward some awaiting receptacles and let them fill up.

If this isn't working, create a rain catcher from a tarpaulin or some plastic sheeting. Lay out your tarp or plastic on the ground, and hunt down about four good-sized sticks and a rock or two. Stretch the tarp between the sticks, and dig the sticks into the ground. Place the rock in the center to help angle the tarp so that rain landing there has an easy channel to drain down to the awaiting bucket.

Dew

These tiny water droplets can be a surprisingly reliable source of water if you can rise early enough in the morning and exercise some patience in harvesting them. Lay a water-absorbent material, like a towel or a shirt, over some grass in the early morning, before the dew evaporates with the coming day. The material will immediately suck up the water that has accumulated on the grass through the night. From here, simply wring out the water into a cup.

Extracting water from plants

In every green plant, no matter the landscape, there exists a potential source of water, whether in the plant itself or in the surrounding soil. Plants need water just as much as humans do, so you can count on any place that supports plant life to also yield water. There may not be gallons and gallons of it, but there will be enough to wet your whistle and keep you going until you come across a more substantial source.

To extract water from the stem or leaves, first cut these sections from the plant and then mash into a wet, fibrous mass in your hand. Clenched tight in your fist, this pulpy lump will soon begin to release its potable liquid, which will trickle out and can be collected in your camp cup or water bottle. Although it may be a little bitter, it's water nonetheless.

Plant roots can also be good sources of water. To get this water from underground, just dig up and pry the roots from the ground below the plant or tree you've selected. Once the roots are out of the ground, chop them into manageable pieces and then mash them against a rock with another rock, making sure to place a container below to catch the bountiful liquid as it's released.

Some water-bearing plants and their parts

Banana or plantain tree—Cut down a tree just above ground level, leaving about 6 inches (15 cm) of the trunk exposed. Hollow out the center of this stump, and watch as water seeps from the roots into the hole you've just created.

Palm tree—Fronds will yield some water if cut and turned upside down to drain.

Bamboo stalk—Cut a notch at the top of a section, and bend the stalk over. Tie it in this downward position, and let the water drain out from the cut. Both old and young bamboo are good sources of water.

Pitcher plant *Nepenthes*—Shaped like its name indicates, this plant holds water in its base to catch insects, so be sure to strain the water unless you want a little bug protein with your drink.

Condensation stills

Another method of procuring water is by harnessing the invisible water vapor that is actually all around us, suspended in the air, and turning it into water droplets in a process known as condensation. Both soil and plants will yield these vapors to varying degrees. Plants, when alive and healthy, give off water vapor during photosynthesis. And soil will also emit good water vapor when its temperature is manipulated by the sun.

Sweating plants

Every method for collecting water through condensation calls for some form of plastic, either a sheet of it or, in the case of a branch (or bag), a simple food baggie. Find some thriving trees with healthy-looking branches, and tie a few bags tightly around the ends of a few different branches. The water vapor in the branches and leaves will heat up inside the plastic and condense as water on the inside of the bag. Check on these bags over the course of a day or two; when done correctly, these bags can yield as much as half a pint (280 ml) of water a day. Simply untie them and drink away!

This method can also work on the ground with low-lying plants and shrubs. Tent these with plastic, using a stick forced into the ground in the center of the plant to keep the plastic away from the greens. At the bottom, curl the plastic in to create large reservoirs for the water to accumulate in, and place some stones on the inside of the plastic to weigh it down.

Freshly gathered greens from trees or plants can also be tented in the same way. First dig a shallow hole in the ground, then dig down around the outer edge of the shallow hole to create a small gully. Place the bag into the shallow center hole, tenting it up with a stick in the ground like the previous example, then fill that area with fresh gathered greenery. Next place the stones in the gully. Curl the plastic under the stones as per the previous example, and this is where the water accumulates after the bag has been sealed and has had a chance to sweat for a few days. To get at the water, just untie the bag, carefully remove the stick and stones, poke a hole in the bag, and drain it like a teabag into your water container.

Sweating soil

This technique is a proven way to get water from the ground by digging a hole. As the soil on the hole's walls heats up, the water vapor present condenses on the cooler plastic on top of the hole, and this then drains into a container.

YOU WILL NEED

✓ Plastic sheeting, or a plastic rain parka

✓ Dozen rocks

✓ Bucket or camp cup

✓ Shovel

STEPS

1 Dig a hole 3 feet (90 cm) deep and about 4 feet (120 cm) wide.

2 Place your bucket or cup in the bottom of the hole.

3 Spread plastic sheeting across the hole, and weigh it down with rocks around the edge of the hole.

4 Place a smaller rock in the center of the plastic so it weighs it down and makes the plastic hover just above the container.

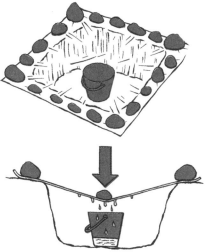

It's possible to exhaust a solar still hole, so in this event just dig another hole and start again, or even better, have a few of these going at once to maximize your water-making effort.

Arid places

Nothing is quite as challenging as tracking down water in a desert environment, but rest assured that it is there. It just takes a little more sleuthing than in other settings.

Look for areas where it appears water has been before or would have pooled during rain, like pockets or depressions in the ground, and try digging down into these for water. The low point between two sand dunes can be a spot where water may have once accumulated. Look also for rock formations, as they can sometimes be hiding water in their nooks and crannies. The more porous the rock the better, as it will have more places for water to pool and collect, so if you see lava rock or limestone, there's a good chance water is there waiting for you. Finally, the rule stated in the beginning of this chapter goes for the desert as well: where there's green vegetation, there's water.

Reviving dried-up water holes

Dry riverbeds can be an unexpectedly good source of water, as they may still have water just under the surface or may have accumulated water after the last rainfall. When attempting this, go for the outside bend of the river as opposed to the inside bend. Dig down a few feet, and see if the hole becomes damp; if indeed it does, then you know water is present and with just a bit more digging you'll be quaffing it in no time.

Some good desert plants and trees for water

Acacia tree *Acacia*—This has a good source of water in its roots, which are low lying and easily accessible.

Baobab *Adansonia digitata*—These roots contain water and are also edible.

Barrel cactus *Ferocactus*—Carefully cut the top off this cactus, and with a stick, mash the innards of the flesh into a pulpy liquid. Insert a hollow reed or grass stem down into it and drink the cactus liquid.

Prickly pear cactus *Opuntia*—The fleshy leaves of this cactus can yield some liquid when chewed on. Mind the needles, though.

Permanent water sources

After a few weekend sojourns into the great outdoors you'll probably be considering a longer stay, and in order to keep yourself properly watered, you'll need to be a bit more proficient in hunting out water. Brush up on the following skills, and you'll never want for a drop.

Springs

Any place where groundwater flows up naturally from an underground source is a spring. Some springwaters have bubbles, and some are flat; some only run during certain times of the year, while others are constantly pouring out their water into a pool or an awaiting stream. Remember that as water makes its way up through the ground, it's picking up traces of minerals as it slips through and over various kinds of rocks, so after you collect it in your container, be sure to purify it.

Rivers

Having a river at your disposal when out in the wild is an ideal situation. If you can, try to collect river water where it moves a little quicker, toward the center of the river, away from the banks where it has a greater chance of pooling and growing stagnant. If you see cattails or rushes growing in parts of the river or spy any foamy bubbles around, steer clear of these areas as a water source—there's a pretty good chance they're contaminated.

Seawater

When you are staying along the beach for a long spell, seawater can provide you with an ample supply of potable water. But you need to get rid of the salt first. One method involves digging just above the high-water mark on the beach and letting the seawater fill the hole. If any freshwater is available in the surrounding sand, it will seep into the hole and sit on top of the denser seawater. Other methods involve using distillation and more condensation processes in order to take the salt out of the seawater (see page 68).

How to build a saltwater still

YOU WILL NEED

✓ Saltwater

✓ Two large metal containers

✓ Plastic sheeting

✓ Plastic tubing

✓ Knife

✓ Tape

✓ Fire

STEPS

1 Fill one large metal container halfway with seawater, cover it tightly with plastic, and seal with tape.

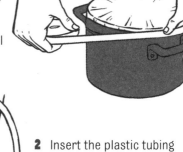

2 Insert the plastic tubing into this container and tightly seal it with tape.

TIP: Keep the tubing from touching the seawater.

3 Seal the second container with plastic and tape, and run the other end of the tube into it. This container will catch the freshwater.

4 Light a fire under the container with the seawater. As it gets hot and boils, the steam it gives off will be salt free and will condense on the tubing and run into the other container, from which you can drink. Keep the fire burning and keep adding seawater, and you'll have clean water in no time.

TIP: If possible, try to place the container that holds the seawater a little higher than the one that will collect the freshwater. This subtle force of gravity can speed things up a bit.

How to dig a well

Most wells these days are drilled with heavy machinery, but if you decide to live long term in a wild place, you may not be able to get those services to your property. In that case you'll be doing the digging yourself with a shovel and pickax.

Digging a well may not be as laborious as it sounds, since it all depends on how far down in the ground the water table is: the shorter that distance the less you have to dig, but in areas with good drainage and low rainfall, you'll be digging a while. It might be worthwhile to hire a company to test the depth of the water table on your property. This is a great time-saver and easier on your back—you won't have to pick random spots, frustrating yourself as you come up dry.

YOU WILL NEED

- ✓ Shovel
- ✓ Pickax
- ✓ Digging pole, pry bar, or steel rod
- ✓ Rope
- ✓ Two planks of wood 2 x 4 inches (5 x 10 cm) thick
- ✓ Rocks, stones, or bricks
- ✓ Two buckets

STEPS

1 Once the magic spot is selected, start digging straight down.

2 Make the mouth of the well a bit larger than the circumference of the actual shaft and remember to allow yourself enough room inside the well to move around and dig. Both circle- and square-shaped wells work fine.

3 When you hit a layer of rock, carefully use the digging rod to break it up. Use the bucket to haul out the dirt collected.

4 Eureka! Once the ground at your feet grows a little damp, wait for more water to seep into the well. When you have a foot (30 cm) of water, place some rocks in the bottom of the well to act as filters.

> **TIP:** You may want to place rocks, starting at the bottom of the well, into the surrounding earth to help fortify the walls. The rocks can also keep dirt from falling into your water source.

If the well becomes deeper than you are tall, it becomes a two-person job, requiring the following extra steps:

5 Stack stones or rocks outside on the lip of the well, place a plank across it, and then secure the plank.

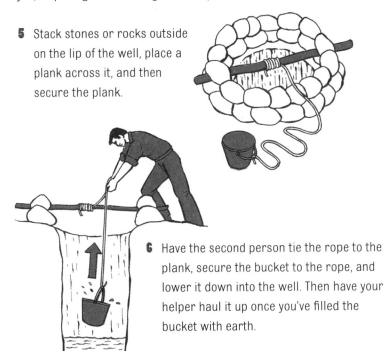

6 Have the second person tie the rope to the plank, secure the bucket to the rope, and lower it down into the well. Then have your helper haul it up once you've filled the bucket with earth.

Making water safe

Before you imbibe—no matter how pure the water looks, whether pulled from a high mountain stream or taken from the mouth of a pristine spring—make sure to first filter and purify it, or you run the risk of inflicting some serious damage to your body.

There are various pump kits on the market that combine a filter and a purifier all in one. They range in size from the mini-portable variety made for backpacking to larger-scale models that run on generators or electricity for a long-term stay in the wild.

Filtering is the first stage of cleaning your water, which removes the larger particles present in whatever you've collected, and should always be followed by purification. If you are without a filtering/purifying pump, filtering can be achieved through some rudimentary means. Simply by letting whatever water you've collected just stand still for 12 hours you'll see the mud, sand, and silt separate from it and gather at the bottom of the container. Pouring the water through material such as your cotton shirt or socks will also work to filter out the bigger particles.

Purification is the last step before you quench that thirst. Almost all purifiers sold for outdoor living work on the method of pumping the water through various chemicals in order to treat it and make it safe for drinking. Iodine and chlorine are the chemicals of choice for purification, whether inside your purification pump or in tablet form, and each chemical flavors the water with its own unique taste. The tablet form is easy to use when out on the trail: just pop the recommended dose into your canteen of newly collected water and let it go to work. The swimming-pool taste or strange color that some tablets might give off shouldn't be seen as a drawback. The fever, chills, and abdominal pains you'll get if you don't use the tablets should.

When out of tablets, or if your pump has suddenly gone kaput, you can always rely on the tried and true method of boiling. Make sure you boil water for at least ten minutes, which is enough to get rid of most harmful organisms.

Transporting water

Besides making you feel like you're part of some ancient fable about persistence, the act of carrying water from the nearby stream to your camp in your bare hands will take an eternity. Simple water containers are an essential piece of gear to take with you into the outdoors, and depending on terrain, chances are you'll want more than one.

Water containers come in all shapes and sizes, and some, like the metal vacuum variety, can perform double duty by keeping cold things cold and hot things hot. Plastic versus metal is kind of a draw, as both have their pros and cons: metal is virtually unbreakable but a little bulky and heavy, while plastic, although lightweight, can be easily punctured. For a lightweight and durable carrier, the collapsible varieties are best. These come in various materials and forms, like nylon bags, large canvas buckets, and the famed Spanish leather wineskins known as bota bags, used by many a mountaineer. The collapsible containers are great, because they can be folded up when not in use and only take up the space in your pack of the amount of water they're holding. Another great option, built for mobility, are the water-holding backpacks, which sport a tube that runs over your shoulder so you can drink as you trek.

If you're without any of the aforementioned containers, Mother Nature has a couple you can turn into makeshift water carriers. The gourd family of plants yield fruits that are perfectly shaped to carry water. Just cut the top off one of these, scrape away the flesh inside, let it dry out, and you've got a good natural jug. Bamboo is ideal for making camp cups, because it grows in hollow segments each blocked off from the next by joints. Just hack a thick bamboo stem down about an inch (2.5 cm) below the top joint and then again just below the bottom joint to create a natural cup.

Storing water

-- -- -- -- -- -- -- -- -- -- -- -- -- -- -- -- --

For long-term stays in the wilderness, storing water is as important as finding water; one never knows when one will come across a good source, so it's good to squirrel away some water and have a backup supply waiting just in case.

Buckets with lids, the 5-gallon (20-liter) type, store water well and have handles so they're mobile if need be. Water troughs, or reservoirs, are simple methods of storage that can be executed with minimal work. This technique is similar to well digging, but doesn't require nearly as much effort since you only need to dig down about 1–2 feet (30–60 cm). Having a few of these going at the same time can really help when water is hard to come by. And if you happen to sense rain, pull the covers off these and let them fill up.

Making a water reservoir

YOU WILL NEED
✓ Shovel   ✓ Rocks
✓ Plastic sheeting

STEPS

1 Start by outlining the circumference of your reservoir with your shovel. Six feet (1.8 m) wide is a good size. If possible, pick a location in the shade, as water exposed to constant sunlight will turn green from algae quicker than water that is covered or shaded. If no shade is to be found, dig a smaller circumference and create a lid from wood or dense foliage to cover it.

2 Dig down to a depth of 2 feet (60 cm) and then flatten down the dirt on the floor of the reservoir.

3 Spread the plastic over the hole, lining the walls and ground, then place the rocks on the outer lip to prevent the plastic from slipping in on itself.

4 Fill it with collected water. Always filter and purify your water before drinking it—you never know what particles may have contaminated it.

TIP: Cover your reservoir with more sheeting weighed down with stones. This will keep out dirt and discourage other wildlife from "sharing" your supplies.

CHAPTER 4

Fire

Living in the woods without fire is like going to a job interview in shorts: it can be done, but your chances are better when you're more prepared. Fire will keep you warm and your socks dry. Fire is also a light in the darkness—great for keeping wild animals and biting insects at bay. You can cook with it, sterilize water with it, and use it to make signals if you're lost. It's also a good mood-setter. Light a fire, find a good poking stick, and then stare into those magical flames and ponder your happy new life in the great outdoors.

Tips, tricks, and tinder

There are plenty of campers who take pride in the one-match fire. Real adventurers take pride in the no-match fire. Next to finding food and water, knowing how to build an efficient and lasting blaze is an essential part of living in the woods.

If you want to get technical, there are three things a fire needs: air, heat, and fuel. You don't have to worry about supplying the air, but you do have to know how to build a fire so that enough air gets to its center. Conversely, too much air, like gusts or gales of wind, won't do you any good either. If you haven't yet built your log cabin, you're going to have to consider the direction of the wind when constructing a campfire.

You will have to supply the heat. Matches are usually the best way to make heat, unless yours are wet. That's when those waterproof matches come in handy. Without such wonderful advances in modern technology at your disposal, you're going to need to know how to coax fire from two rocks or by rubbing two sticks together (more on this later).

Getting the right fuel is up to you as well. Just finding a few big pieces of wood isn't going to cut it. You need small kindling first—those really small twigs that are extra dry and would catch fire with nothing more than a match. Then you need bigger kindling (wood that's no thicker than a pencil). Then you should have small pieces of wood and, finally, your bigger pieces. But you can't just burn any wood you find. Some burns too fast, some burns too slow, and some doesn't burn at all (more on this later, too).

Tinder is another very important part of campfire fuel—some say the most important part. If you don't have matches, you can't build a fire without it. This is what gets the initial flame going from the sparks of a flint stone or the friction from rubbing two sticks together. If you do have matches, then lighting tinder at the center of a well-constructed fire can get even damp kindling burning. Luckily, nature supplies us with many different kinds of tinder—just make sure it's dry, dry, dry.

There is some tinder that needs a bit of preparation to be at its combustible best. If you're having trouble finding dry tinder, you can rub it on dry, absorbent cotton clothing. Another way to dry tinder is to keep it in your pockets, as long as those pockets are cotton; body heat will help dry it out. In fact, even at the risk of appearing like a homeless pack rat with overstuffed pockets, it's not a bad idea to squirrel away tinder when you find it. You can never have enough.

For bark and wood shavings, rub the tinder between your hands or against a dry rock surface. This will turn the tinder into a fine fluff, which is good for friction fire lighting (rubbing two sticks together). If you happen to run across some bracket fungi, cut it open to get to the fluffy layer under the hard outer crust.

Charred cotton or silk cloth can be made (ahead of time if possible) by setting it on fire and then stamping it out when it turns dark brown or black. This is excellent tinder if you're using a flint stone or other sparking source. Once the cloth is charred, though, it has to be kept dry.

Tinder nature tenders

Bark, especially birch bark and the shredded inner bark from chestnut, cedar, and red elm trees, is nature's tinder. Look for stalks from old grass, tree flowers, and fruits. Other good tinder includes:

✓ Bird down

✓ Cotton fluff

✓ Dry grass or straw

✓ Dead pine needles

✓ Sawdust

✓ Wood shavings

✓ Lint from pockets or seams

✓ Dead bracken or fern leaves

✓ Bracket fungi, which is often found growing on the trunks of dying trees

✓ Charred cotton or silk cloth

Fire safety

While having a campfire is one of the essentials of backwoods living, it can turn bad in a hurry if you're not careful. Because of this, there are some essential safety guidelines to keep in mind as you're collecting your tinder and firewood.

Lots of national parks and wilderness areas limit fires to preexisting fire pits and to certain areas of the park. They do this for good reasons. Always follow park guidelines when it comes to fires. You can get fined, kicked out, or both.

Check drought and fire conditions, especially during summer months. Often local law enforcement agencies will post fire conditions, and most locals will be able to advise—just ask. A single spark from a campfire can burn down hundreds of acres of forest in a matter of days.

Always build a fire on bare earth, so the fire will do no obvious damage to the location. Whenever camping, you want to leave as little trace of your stay as possible.

If you're on the move, be sure your campfire is completely extinguished before you leave. Do this by spreading out the coals and letting the fire die down. Then pour water on it. Don't be shy with the water; it needs to soak into the ground to make sure any underground roots aren't smoldering (this does happen). Lastly, spread the coals farther apart with your hands (if they're still too hot to touch, use more water). Then brush over the fire site with a branch to hide the fact that you were ever there.

TIP: Never burn poison oak or ivy, or even wood that's been touching these itchy plants. The smoke itself can cause an allergic rash.

Firewood

It would be nice to report that wood is wood and that all of it burns. Wishful thinking. Not only do you need to pay attention to what kind of firewood you collect, but you have to make sure that you get the right sizes of wood, from kindling to major logs. And whatever wood you gather, be sure to get plenty of it before setting your fire ablaze, or you'll be tramping through the darkness searching for more.

Deadwood and trees already felled are drier and more ready to burn than trees you have to chop down. In any case, most national and state parks won't let you chop down trees for firewood. When searching for already felled wood, try to find wood that's been caught or snagged in branches above the ground rather than wood that's on the ground, which will contain more moisture. As a general rule, hardwoods like oak burn the hottest and longest, while softwoods like pine burn bright and fast. Greenwood—wood that hasn't had a chance to dry out—usually smokes more than it burns. For that matter, any wood that's wet is no good. Rotten wood won't burn either.

Any fire you might want to cook with should be made from only clean wood. Plastics, fire lighters, or fence posts coated with pitch will impart a nasty flavor to your roast dinner, and smoke from poisonous plants or weeds can make you ill.

Alternatives to wood

✓ Dried grasses twisted into bunches   ✓ Dried animal dung

✓ Coal   ✓ Dry peat moss

✓ An old pair of socks

Building a fire

Now to the fun part. Once you've collected and stored plenty of tinder, kindling, and firewood, it's time to get a blaze going. Unless there's a fire pit already in place for you, you'll have to prepare one yourself. Generally, fires should be in areas that are relatively out of the wind and well away from low-hanging limbs and dry grasses. Before you get started, clear a circle about 6 feet (1.8 m) in diameter of any underbrush and preferably scrape the spot down to bare soil. Then dig a shallow pit 6 inches (15 cm) deep at the center of the circle.

All fires should start with the same thing: a grapefruit-sized ball of dry fluffy tinder on a bed of small kindling, surrounded by more small kindling. The three most common types of fire lays are the teepee, the pyramid or crisscross, and the star fire.

Teepee fire

This is the most standard campfire lay of all. It can be used on its own or to start other types of fires. Fire naturally burns upward, and the chimney shape of this construction causes the smoke to funnel up as well.

STEPS

1 Build a bed of small kindling, tinder, and extra small kindling in the center of the pit.

2 With pencil-shaped pieces of kindling, begin making a small but tight teepee over the tinder bed.

3 Build the teepee out using gradually larger and larger pieces of wood, but don't use pieces that are thicker than your wrist. The teepee fire is notoriously unstable when built with large, heavy pieces of wood.

4 Use larger logs to surround the teepee in a square.

5 Once the teepee of wood is constructed, light the tinder at its center.

Pyramid or crisscross fire

Pyramid fires are good cooking fires. They're also long lasting.

STEPS

1 Place 2–3 large logs next to each other over the fire pit, and lay somewhat smaller logs across these to form the pyramid base.

2 Continue layering logs perpendicular to the layer beneath, with each layer using smaller pieces of wood.

3 Stop after about six layers or when you have a small, flat platform at the top of the pyramid.

4 Using the instructions on page 82, build a teepee fire on top of the platform and light it. The fire will burn downward.

Star fire

This type of fire is a traditional Native American construction. It uses little wood and can last for days, making it a good fire for a permanent camp.

STEPS

1 First build a teepee fire at the center of the pit.

2 Place the ends of large logs at the center of the fire, letting their lengths extend out in the shape of a star.

3 Feed these logs into the center of the fire as they burn.

Starting a fire with no matches

Waterproof matches are a trekker's best friend. We recommend carrying several boxes at all times—they're small and can fit into any number of backpack pockets. One good place to stash a few is in your tent—simply leave them inside when you pack it up.

Having said that, if your preparedness is somehow met with unforeseen circumstances (let's say you fall into a raging river and manage to save yourself but all your gear goes over a large waterfall), then all is not lost. You can get warm and dry the old-fashioned way: by getting out your flint stone or by rubbing two sticks together.

The old bow-and-drill trick

When you hear the term "rubbing two sticks together" used with regard to fire lighting, what this really refers to is the bow-and-drill technique. Using this ancient fire-starting method, you achieve heat through friction by drilling a hardwood stick (known as the drill) into a flat piece of wood (known as the hearth), using a bow and string. It's not easy, but it works as long as you're willing to find the right materials and put some energy into the drilling.

YOU WILL NEED

- ✓ A straight stick of hardwood for the drill
- ✓ A flat piece of dry hardwood for the hearth
- ✓ An 18-inch (45-cm) stick of greenwood for the bow
- ✓ A rope, shoelace, or any other piece of tough string
- ✓ A hand-sized piece of hardwood to use as the socket (this is what you'll hold and press down on the drill with when you're turning it)
- ✓ A knife
- ✓ A strong piece of bark
- ✓ Tinder

STEPS

1 Before trying to get a spark from the bow and drill, build yourself a teepee fire lay, but make sure you have easy and direct access to the tinder platform in the middle. Once you get an ember from the drill hearth, you'll need to transfer it quickly to the fire lay.

2 Start making your bow-and-drill setup by whittling one end of the drill into a point. Round off the other end.

3 Cut a small hole halfway along the hearth about an inch (2.5 cm) from an edge. The hole should be big enough to allow the rounded end of the drill to fit inside it.

4 Cut a triangular notch in the hearth from the hole to the nearest edge. This will serve as a channel for ashes and embers to spill out and onto your tinder.

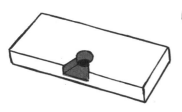

5 You're going to use the socket to press down firmly on the drill. To stop it from slipping, cut a small hole in the socket so that the pointed end of the drill will fit there snugly.

TIP: It's best for the drill and the hearth to be the of same type of wood.

6 Tie the cord or shoelace to the bow. It's helpful to find a bow stick that's already bent, but a green stick should bend naturally as you tie on the string.

7 Place the hearth on the ground so that the notched side is in contact with a small but strong piece of bark (this is where you will collect the embers).

8 Place the rounded end of the drill in the hole on the hearth. Loop the bow cord over the drill, and push down firmly on top of the drill with the socket.

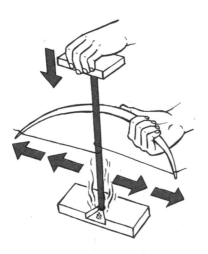

9 Make sawing motions with the bow to work the drill back and forth in a not-too-fast, not-too-slow, steady rhythm. Make sure the drill stays in contact with the hearth.

10 Eventually, the friction will cause smoke to form and dark brown smoking powder should start rolling down the notch and onto the bark. When smoke appears, increase speed and pressure on the drill.

11 Once the notch is filled with smoking powder and the powder is smoking on its own, gently move the hearth away from the bark and smoking powder. Place the smoking powder onto a small but tight ball of tinder, and blow on it until it turns into a glowing red ember. The tinder should also begin to catch fire.

12 Quickly take the smoldering ball of tinder to the teepee fire and place it gently on the tinder platform. Blow on it more if need be until the kindling catches.

Keeping your fire going

Now that the fire is lit, you don't want it to go out. Anyone who has ever worked an ember out of a piece of wood with a bow and drill will stress this point.

One way to prevent it from burning out overnight is to bank the fire. Do this by covering the hot coals with ash. Don't bury the coals under a foot of ash, but do pile on enough so that you can't see anything glowing.

Another good technique to practice as a companion to banking a fire is the wind shield, which can also double as a heat reflector. These crude walls can be constructed out of wrist-sized firewood lashed to two vertical struts and propped up at an angle next to the fire. This will prevent too much wind from blowing directly on the fire and burning it out in a hurry. On cold nights, the surface of the wind shield facing the fire can direct the heat from the fire toward your bivouac or tent. In very windy and cold weather you can build an L-shaped fire wall for increased protection and lots of reflected heat.

Wind shields can also be made out of stacked rocks. Plus, the shallow pit you dug before even building the fire takes the hot center out of any direct wind, making the fire more efficient and preventing it from burning up all your firewood before lunch.

Starting a fire in cold or wet weather

If it's extra cold outdoors, with snow or rain, there's no better time for a crackling warm campfire to get the chill out of your bones. The problem is that it's really hard to build a fire in the pouring rain or when there's snow all over the place. But don't give up—fire is often crucial in this type of weather. Here's what to do:

Platform fire

If there's light snow or ice on the ground, make a double platform by lining up wrist-sized pieces of greenwood, the first layer laying parallel to each other and the second layer running in the opposite direction. This will allow the fire to get going faster than it would on the damp, cold ground.

Raised fire

If the ground is really wet, consider building a raised platform. Drive four sticks into the ground and lash four sticks between the corners to make a square base. Then stack wrist-sized pieces of wood alongside each other to create a flat surface. To prevent the wood platform from burning, use greenwood if possible and put a thick layer of clay or soil under the fire lay.

Fire in rain

Building a fire in the rain can be disheartening. The best way to go about this is to construct a temporary roof over your fire lay. Try building a fire next to a tree stump or large rock that you can use as a base to prop leafy tree branches over the fire like a makeshift lean-to. A rain poncho held up by sticks is another option, though that means you'll get wetter trying to light the fire. The best option is to find large pieces of bark and create a small roof with four corner sticks. That way you don't have to worry when the roof itself catches on fire, which is not the case in the previous two suggestions.

Using a fire for signaling

If you're lost, fire can be a great way to draw attention to yourself. During daylight hours, smoke can be seen for miles around, and airplanes will be better able to spot a fire than, say, you standing there frantically waving your arms back and forth. At night, a fire may be the only way you can signal to would-be rescuers.

How to set up a fire signal

Of course, if you aren't lost, you don't want every park ranger descending on you when the fire gets going. That's why fire signals always come in threes. If you need to set up a fire signal, here's what to do:

STEPS

1 If you're in the woods, find a clearing so that the tree cover won't obscure the fires.

2 Build three teepee fire lays in a triangle about 10 feet (3 m) apart.

3 Use one fire as your everyday campfire. When the need comes to light all three, you'll have to do it quickly.

4 Three columns of smoke is part of the international distress signal. To get smoky fires, use dry wood for kindling but put green or freshly cut trees on top of that.

CHAPTER 5

Food

Your body is a furnace, and food is your fuel. When you're out in the wilderness, that logic goes double, since getting that fuel can sometimes take twice the work. Sure, in the steel-and-concrete confines of the city you can eat whatever and whenever you please, but out in the wild it's a different story altogether. You are no longer the happy-go-lucky customer content in choosing from whatever options are laid out on the menu of the day—necessity dictates that you now play an active role in what and when you eat. If you don't go out and get it, you could starve to death.

Eating out in the woods

The first thing to get into your head is all the different hats you'll be wearing when out in nature. There's no middleman between you and your meals out there, so you'll need to be both butcher and chef, not to mention a stone-cold hunter of meat, fish, and plants (okay, perhaps a forager of that last one there).

Out of all of those, it's probably the hunter and butcher hats that you'll be most nervous to don, and rightfully so. It's okay to be nervous, it's not everyone who can snare a rabbit and skin it for dinner, especially if you're the type who can't even bring yourself to kill a spider that's set up camp in your shower. But a funny thing happens when out in the wild for extended spells: one can only go for so long without that fuel. At a certain point, even the most pacific mind morphs into a cavemanlike mentality, and you simply must have that meat no matter what. This is usually the point where you find yourself frantically whittling a few sticks for a loop snare and then giddily waiting behind a nearby tree for that rascally rabbit to finally saunter on by.

Vegetarians need not despair; it's not all meat out there in the wilderness. There are plenty of tasty greens to choose from, and they're a whole lot easier to sneak up on and subdue than any four-legged animal of the forest. And just think of the oodles of time you'll save: no frustrating hours spent trying to coax a fish onto a hook, just simply bend over and pluck your dinner from the earth. Young shoots, berries, fruits, and the roots of many different plants provide tasty vegetarian options for eating out—in the woods.

And it doesn't all have to be salads and steak tartare: your newfound fire-building skills can be put to good use to craft a surprising variety of home-away-from-home cuisine.

Nutrition and calories

Basic nutrition requires a daily intake of a variety of foods for optimal health, and in the wild a balanced diet is the key to your overall survival. A good wilderness diet should include a healthy mix of carbohydrates, proteins, fats, vitamins, and minerals.

Whether reading the morning newspaper or chopping wood, our bodies are constantly burning calories, which are the basic units of energy in food. Everyone's metabolism is different, but every day there is a calorific intake/activity ratio at work within us that can differ with activity, climate, gender, and age, with each of these factors calling for varying amounts of calories. Believe it or not, staying in bed all day watching TV will burn 2,000 calories, so just imagine how many calories you'll burn hiking out on the trail. In general, the average energy burned by a semiactive man aged 18–35 is anywhere between 2,000 to 3,500 calories a day, but once out in nature the calorific need grows higher as he does more strenuous activity. Likewise with climate: someone trekking in a colder environment, say the Himalayas, will need substantially more calories per day than someone tramping around a warmer area of the globe. The same goes for gender and age: women tend to have a smaller calorific intake than men, and as you age your metabolism slows down and you're not quite as active as you once were.

Not all foods are created equal, so it's important to plan your rations and to pack foods with a high calorie count that will help in maximizing your energy output. Before packing food, consider the following:

★ **Duration of trip**—How long will you be out in the woods?

★ **Activity**—How strenuous?

★ **Weight**—How much weight can you carry on your back? This usually decides what you're taking.

★ **Cooking**—Can your food be cooked over a fire?

Food brought from home

Basic outdoors food can take on a few forms, from canned goods to fresh foods, including dry and wet varieties. This isn't really the place to be adventurous with your palate, so carry what you know you like, and you should be fine.

Canned goods

A wide variety exists here, from main meals that are simple to prepare, like sausages and beans or a hearty chili dish, to fruits in their own juices or veggies in water. They can be eaten cold if necessary. Their main drawback is their weight.

TIP: To lighten the load a bit, just repackage. Take your canned goods out of the can and pack them in lightweight Tupperware or collapsible plastic carrying cases. You'll be surprised at how much lighter this can make your pack.

Fresh foods

There is no harm in carrying fresh fruits, vegetables, or even a cut of meat. The main drawback is they'll expire rapidly in the wild, so they should be consumed first, if packed at all.

Dry foods

In recent years, the average backpacker's dehydrated and freeze-dried meals have gone gourmet. You can get everything from organic wild mushroom and asparagus risotto to pad Thai, or you can just opt for the old standbys like beef Stroganoff or burgers. No real drawbacks here—just be mindful in preparing these meals and allow for the proper water-soaking time. If not, you could run the risk of dehydration as the food will actually absorb the water in your body. Not a very appetizing thought.

Wet foods

Also known as pouched food, wet food is basically any prepared foodstuff stored in a boilable pouch. It is relatively painless to prepare, and there's no mess to clean—just boil water and drop in your pouch, and ten minutes later you've got tandoori chicken. And with the leftover boiled water you can make yourself hot cocoa or break out the honey, brandy, and lemon and get to mixing that hot toddy you so justly deserve. Drawbacks here are the actual pouches—which are prone to puncture—so if you're going this route, make sure you house the pouches in a hard travel case.

Quick bites on the trail

Whether you are in the middle of a hike, needing something to tide you over while trying to prepare a meal in wet and windy conditions, or as a simple dessert, a nutritious snack can make all the difference. Lightweight, high-energy foods that are easy to carry and require no preparation can give you just the boost you need to cover those last few miles back to camp. Try any of the following:

★ **GORP**—Good Old Raisins and Peanuts. This is the original trail mix and can be augmented with other fruits and/or nuts. Almonds and cashews are a great source of fats, and dried fruits like pineapple or apricots are high in vitamins. Throw in some chocolate chips for your sweet tooth.

★ **Canned fish**—Different varieties like sardines in olive oil or tuna in water are good sources of protein.

★ **Crackers**—Got to have something to spread the sardines on, don't you? Also a good carbohydrate supplier, crackers are a better option than bread because crackers won't freeze.

★ **Preserved meat**—Try assorted jerky flavors or even a nice dry salami; these are usually pretty lightweight.

★ **Energy bars**—These are good trail snacks for intermittent nibbling.

Cooking on an open fire

Cooking your meal over an open fire is a quintessential woods experience that can be done lots of different ways, from skewering to boiling.

Skewering

This is cooking at its simplest. Just find a nice sapling and poke it through your fish fillet, rabbit, or small bird, starting at the tail and running it through to where the head was. Hold the meat over the fire, making sure to turn it so it cooks evenly. For fish, you'll know it's done when the skin gets flaky.

One-pot cooking

As the name suggests, this is cooking with one pot. Generally, this is when you're looking to boil something—perhaps a rabbit you've snared—and you want to cook it along with some vegetables or other flavorings. One-pot cooking is done with the use of a spit, whereby you dangle a pot filled with water and meat over the fire at a certain height and wait for your scrumptious stew to do its thing.

Making a one-pot spit

YOU WILL NEED

✓ A cooking pot

✓ A rock

✓ Two long, sturdy branches/sticks

✓ Two forked branches

STEPS

1 Let a nice-sized fire burn down a bit to reveal some hot embers.

2 On opposite sides of the fire, dig the two forked branches into the ground, or hammer them in with a rock.

3 Place your sturdy branch/stick across the fire, setting it into the forks of the branches.

4 Fill your pot with its intended meal and slide it onto one side of the horizontal branch. With your second stick in hand, guide the pot into prime position over the heart of the fire, and try to be patient as the aroma of your stew fills the forest.

Roasting

A favored method of cooking meat for many an adventurer is roasting. This method differs from the one-pot spit only in that instead of threading a pot onto the stick, you thread your kill onto the stick. In making this spit, be sure to choose branches that can sustain the weight of your kill.

TIP: Using twine and a short stick, you can make a handle on the end of the long branch to aid in rotating the meat for even cooking. Just make a "T" with the short stick on the end of the long branch and secure it with twine.

Baking fish in mud

If you've run out of aluminum foil, this is your method of choice. Start by making a fire, then gather some large green leaves. Overlap your leaves, and place your fish in the center of them. Wrap the fish tightly with the leaves. Now encase the entire unit in a thick layer of mud. Once your fire has burned down to hot embers, you can place your mud-fish package on top. Lastly, you need to start a small fire on top of the fish, so you'll need to make a thick layer of light kindling and wood on top of the mud-fish and then light it. Let it burn down, and in about an hour the mud will have hardened. You can then take the mud-fish out and crack off the dried mud, revealing a nicely moist baked fish inside.

The Yukon stove

While a bit more of a challenge, creating cooking apparatuses from the earth has many advantages—longevity and increased heat production being the main strengths. With the Yukon stove, which is essentially a chimney built over a fire, you can keep warm, dry wet wood, and cook dinner. It takes a bit of effort, but once built it can burn almost anything.

YOU WILL NEED

✓ A shovel

✓ Stones in a range of sizes

✓ Firewood

✓ Mud, clay, or earth

STEPS

1 Start by digging a nice-sized hole with your shovel, say a foot (30 cm) round and a foot (30 cm) deep.

2 On one side of the hole, etch out a channel that leads down to the hole. Since this is where you'll be feeding the fire its fuel, make sure it's big enough to fit the wood you'll be employing.

3 Erect a teepee fire (see page 82) in the hole, but don't light it just yet.

4 With your larger rocks, begin building around the hole to eventually create a funnel/pyramid shape. Make sure to span the channel with one large rock, and then start to narrow the funnel shape with each successively smaller layer of rock as you near the top.

5 Once near the top, widen out a bit, creating a bigger opening, or mouth, to the funnel.

6 Once you have a rough pyramid, patch any open spaces with mud or clay and let it harden for an airtight seal.

7 Light a small piece of kindling or a stick, and send it through the channel to ignite your teepee.

8 As the fire burns, the oven will start to heat throughout. You can control the temperature by regulating the opening at the top of the funnel. Feed the fire by adding firewood through the channel or by carefully dropping it in through the funnel's top.

9 You've got some options for cooking with the Yukon stove. Place a grate on top of the opening to grill a steak, or leave skewered meat hanging over the opening. You can also wait for the fire to recede to embers and tuck a wrapped piece of meat through the channel for a nice baked meal.

Survival skills: easy meals

- -

Having consumed the last of your food just after sunup, the idea of tramping through the woods in search of food, whether plant, mammal, or anywhere in between, can seem a daunting experience. It doesn't have to be. Inside each one of us lies a dormant hunter/gatherer, so we're hardwired to do this. It's just that most of us don't know how or where to start.

When foraging for plants, the line between what you can eat and what you can't eat can at times be difficult to distinguish. What looks like watercress to your eyes could very well make you quite sick if you ingest it. When it comes to animals, the "thrilling" hunt that some folks talk about can sometimes take days to accomplish, leaving you quite tuckered out and reeling at the thought of having to now prepare the meat for consumption. And as far as the anywhere in between, who really wants to dine on grasshoppers and lizards if you don't have to, right? Well, there may come a time when you just have to.

Animals you can eat

★ **Invertebrates/insects**—Snails, slugs, worms. Worms are a great source of protein; squeeze them from top to tail and then roast or fry to taste. Termites, grasshoppers, beetles, and grubs are also good sources of protein and benefit tremendously from roasting.

★ **Amphibians**—Salamanders, newts, and frogs are obviously more appetizing when fried or roasted.

★ **Reptiles**—You have to catch more than a couple of lizards for a substantial meal, but once roasted they can be quite good.

★ **Birds**—Virtually all birds are edible. Ducks, geese, or quail slow-cooked over fire is best. And don't forget the eggs.

★ **Mammals**—Many varieties exist. Deer, rabbit, and wild boar are old wilderness staples.

★ **Fish**—Will taste great cooked over a fire.

Animals you can't eat

★ **Invertebrates/insects**—Avoid any brightly colored ones, spiders, ticks, flies, caterpillars, and generally anything too hairy or that can bite or sting.

★ **Amphibians**—Stay away from toads, as most secrete a poison under their skin, and any brightly colored frog with an "X" on its back.

★ **Reptiles**—In general don't bother with snakes. They are creepy and too hard to catch.

★ **Mammals**—Beware the scavenging mammals, such as raccoons or opossums.

Nature's salad bar: plants as food

Run out of food on the trail? Never fear. Mother Nature has provided the adventurer with a bountiful harvest. Trees, plants, and their many parts can sustain a life in the wild for long stretches of time.

HOW TO PERFORM A TASTE TEST

If you stumble upon a shrub that looks enough like arugula to eat, resist the temptation to gobble it up and test the plant to be sure it's edible. Make sure you test only one part of the plant at a given time, and don't ingest anything else for the duration of the test.

STEPS

1 **Smell**—Crush a leaf, and if it smells like peaches or almonds, discard it.

2 **Skin contact**—Take that newly crushed leaf and hold it to the inside of your forearm for about ten minutes. If there's any reaction, like a rash or burning, don't eat it. If you have no reaction at all, proceed with the test.

3 **Mouth contact**—Place a small amount of the leaf on your tongue for a few minutes and wait for a reaction. If nothing happens, then chew that amount but don't swallow it, and keep it in your mouth for 15 minutes. If no numbness or burning exists, go to the next step.

4 **Swallow**—Swallow what you have in your mouth and gauge the effects for five hours. If you don't suffer adverse reactions, then the plant is okay.

Plants you can eat

★ **Acacia** *(Acacia)*—Tree with spiky branches and small compound leaves. Shoots and leaves are edible after boiling, and the seeds can be roasted for a snack. An arid-area tree, its roots can be tapped as a source of water.

★ **Baobab** *(Adansonia digitata)*—Tree with short branches and a large fruit resembling a football. Fruit is edible raw, as are young leaves. Root contains water and is edible as well.

★ **Blackberries** *(Rubus)*—Dark red to black fruit; mind the thorns on the vine. Wash and eat raw. Beware, though—blackberries are often sprayed with herbicide in areas where they grow as weeds.

★ **Bracken** *(Pteridium aquilinum)*—Large leaf, grows in clumps. The young shoots can be boiled. Roots can be roasted.

★ **Cattail** *(Typha)*—Long narrow leaves, tubelike flower. Boil leaves or rootstock.

★ **Chicory** *(Cichorium intybus)*—All parts are edible, from the young leaves to the root. Great stand-in for coffee—just roast the roots brown, crush them to a powder, and enjoy a mug of chicory.

★ **Dandelion** *(Taraxacum)*—Long, jagged leaves. Young leaves can be consumed raw. Roots can be boiled.

★ **Garden sorrel** *(Rumex acetosa)*—Long leaves, small red-and-green flowers. Leaves can be consumed raw but may benefit from boiling.

★ **Juniper** *(Juniperus communis)*—Small berries, a bluish-black when ripe. Wash and eat raw.

★ **Oak** *(Quercus)*—Acorns. Shell them and boil twice, then roast and eat.

★ **Pigweed** *(Amaranthus)*—Basil-like leaf. Blanch leaves and stem in boiling water, like you would spinach. Shoots can be eaten raw.

★ **Primrose** *(Primula)*—Wrinkled leaves, five-petaled flowers. Boil leaves and eat.

★ **Walnut** *(Juglans)*—Consume raw nut, or roast it.

Plants you can't eat

★ **Belladonna** *(Atropa belladonna)*—Also called "deadly nightshade," which says it all. Dull green leaves and purple bell-shaped flowers with black shiny berries.

★ **Buttercup** *(Ranunculus)*—Don't let the name fool you. Yellow flower with five glossy overlapping petals.

★ **Death camas** *(Zigadenus)*—Another not-so-subtle name. Long leaves and white flowers.

★ **Foxglove** *(Digitalis)*—Distinctive bell-shaped flowers, colors vary from white, yellow, pink, and purple.

★ **Fungi**—Not so fun if you pick the wrong variety to dine on. Unless you're 100 percent sure of the species or happen to be a mycologist, stay away from mushrooms as food, as too many edible varieties look identical to the poisonous ones.

★ **Hemlock** *(Conium maculatum)*—White umbrellalike flowers.

★ **Lantana** *(Lantana camara)*—Shrublike plant with fruit resembling blackberries.

★ **Lupine** *(Lupinus)*—Star-shaped leaves with a purple, pink, or white flower.

★ **Oleander** *(Nerium oleander)*—Shrub/tree with variously colored flowers, from white to red to pink.

★ **Poison ivy/oak** *(Toxicodendron)*—Don't even touch this one. "Leaves of three, let them be"—heed this old warning. Various colors from red to green depending on the season.

> **TIP:** Think twice. While it is true there are more edible than poisonous plants out there, there is still a level of concern that must be observed when foraging for plants in the wild. If any one section of a plant is poisonous, then chances are the rest of it probably is too. For the most part try to avoid any plants with fine hairs or thorns, and any that have a milky white sap.

Fishing

"Give a man a fish and you feed him for a day, teach a man to fish and you feed him for a lifetime." As far as adages go, this one is right on the gill. Fish is an ideal food when out in the woods. Packed with protein and essential vitamins and fats, fish can provide a tasty treat for those with the skill and patience to catch them.

Line fishing

Getting started on line fishing requires only a few fundamental items, namely a rod, reel, some tackle, and a good bit of luck. Should you find yourself with none of the above, don't despair. Mother Nature is at your service. For a rod, you basically just need any strong branch or sapling, preferably one that is about your general height or a bit longer. Give it a bend test to make sure it's going to hold up if you land the big one. If you've got twine or any kind of rope in your pack, get it. If not, see pages 25–27 and make some. Then make a hook and a float and gather some bait.

HOOKS

TRY ONE OF THESE

✓ Nails

✓ Safety pins

✓ Wire

✓ Key rings or backpack buckles

✓ Any thorny stem

Just bend any of the above into the rough shape of a hook. If using stems, cut a section of branch, roughly the size of your finger, from a thorny bramble bush, preferably one with large thorns, and cut a notch in the end opposite the thorn/hook to tie your line to.

FLOATS

Floats will help you see when the fish are actually biting and will keep your hook at the desired depth for whichever environment you're fishing. Given the name, you can fashion these from anything that floats.

```
TRY ONE OF THESE
✓  Cork                    ✓  Nutshells
✓  Tree bark               ✓  Any brightly colored berries
```

For each of these, just thread your line through the center of the float, leaving enough line below for your hook to dangle at the desired depth. Then make knots below and above the float to hold it in place.

BAIT

If you can find a worm, more power to you. If not, you'll have to figure out another way to trick your dinner into biting that hook.

```
TRY ONE OF THESE
✓  Insects: grubs, grasshoppers, etc.    ✓  Cheese
✓  Berries                               ✓  Pasta
✓  Bread                                 ✓  Corn
```

Remember to pay attention to your surroundings. More often than not, fish dine on the insects and vegetation of their immediate locale. If you use something they're used to for bait, your chances of landing a fish for dinner improve dramatically.

Spearfishing

Spearing is an alternative way, albeit more physical, to get some fish. But in order to get the most out of it, you should do it in fairly shallow water, about knee-deep, and make sure that the fish you're after are of a good enough size to warrant your effort.

Spears are fairly easy to come by, unless you happen to be in the desert— but then you won't be doing any fishing there, will you? Just find a long, sturdy branch and whittle it to a fine point. Make sure your spear is longer than the depth of the water you're looking to make your kill in. Then get to work.

SPEARING TECHNIQUE

1 From the riverbank, slide the tip of your spear slowly into the water where you think fish are gathering. You need to keep at least the point in the water at all times, as this allows for a quicker initial strike and avoids a splash that could scare your fish away.

2 Keep in mind that water refracts light, so when you eventually spot your trout dinner idling near a boulder, you'll probably need to aim a little lower in the water in order to actually get it.

3 Once you have it pinned, don't attempt to bring it out on the spear— it may wriggle off. Hold it in the water and use a net or your hands to bring it out of the river.

TIP: Here are a few casting secrets. Patience is most definitely a virtue. Approach your spot on the river quietly. Remember, you're hunting. Most fish love the shade, so anything that casts a shadow or a dark area in the water is a prime fish-gathering area. If you see your float bob just a hair or feel a tug on your rod, no matter how slight, react quickly by pulling up on your rod to set the hook. Finally, pull your meal carefully to shore.

The bottle trap

This trick won't land the big one, but what it lacks in size it makes up for in quantity, as groups of little fish go in but they can't find their way out.

STEPS

You are going to need a knife, large plastic bottle, and some good bait in order to successfully set your bottle trap.

1 Make an incision about 4 inches (10 cm) from the mouth and cut the bottle in two parts, leaving the base at least three times bigger than the top.

2 Fill the bigger base section with bait—cheese, bread, etc.

3 Invert the top into the bigger base section and place the trap in the water near the water's edge. Weigh it down with rocks if need be.

4 Sit back and read your book, and remember to check the trap regularly.

Preparing fish

Once you've caught yourself some fish, you need to then prepare them for eating. If it's hot outside, don't dillydally lest supper go bad. By the same token, in cold climates, fish will keep longer and can even be packed in snow to preserve them, as a natural form of quick-freeze (although you'll want to take extra care to cook them thoroughly if you try this).

In general, preparing fish is more messy than difficult. A sharp knife is essential, as larger fish can be pretty tough and even smaller fish are impossible to fillet without proper tools (see pages 22–23 for tips on knives and how to sharpen them). When you're finished, the parts you don't want to eat needn't go to waste. They can be boiled with a few herbs or vegetables to make stock, which when strained makes a good base for soup or even a hot drink for the truly hungry.

You might find yourself a bit squeamish about messing around with the internal organs the first few times, but this will wear off. And if you're cold and hungry enough, the thought of a tasty grilled fillet of trout should help you set aside your qualms.

STEPS

1 Holding the fish by the tail, scrape the scales off by running your knife repeatedly from tail to head at a 45-degree angle away from you.

2 Place your knife at the opening of the fish's anus, making a careful slit from here all the way to just below the gills.

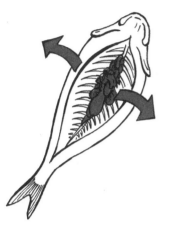

3 Spread the fish open and scoop out all internal organs.

4 Cut off the head, tail, and fins. Save for soup stock if so inclined.

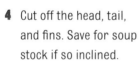

5 With the fish spread before you, separate one side of the ribs from the body with your knife blade. At this point you can probably just lift the whole rib cage out with your bare hands.

6 Take the fillet to the riverside and briefly wash it in the water.

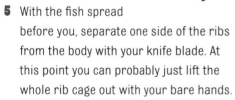

Hunting

Hunting in the wild

When living for a prolonged time in the great outdoors, the hunting of animals will probably become a necessity for your survival. If that sounds like the greatest horror you can imagine, just wait until you haven't eaten for a few days. But even then, don't go on a rampage, killing everything you come across. Be mindful when you're out in nature. Show respect for your prey, and use as much of the animal as you can: meat, hide, etc. In many wilderness areas, hunting is heavily legislated and in some parts it's prohibited outright, so do yourself a favor and check the laws pertaining to your locale, and learn the legal seasons for the various game you'll be hunting.

Weapons in the wild

Are you packing heat? No, not fire—firearms. If you're after game with a gun, use your shots wisely so as not to run out of ammunition too quickly, and remember, safety first. When you run out of bullets or want a more stealthy approach, you'll need to improvise an ancient but accurate weapon, the bow and arrow.

How to make a bow and arrow

YOU WILL NEED

- ✓ A flexible branch
- ✓ Six straight branches
- ✓ A knife
- ✓ String, twine, or rope
- ✓ Feathers

STEPS

1 Choose your flexible branch/bow wood wisely. Make sure it's at least 4 feet (1.2 m) long. Good wood options are oak, willow, elm, and birch.

2 With your knife, whittle the ends of your branch narrow while leaving the middle a bit fatter.

3 Cut notches in both ends of the bow. You will tie your bowstring to these, so make sure they're good grooves.

4 Tie your string around one groove, bend the bow, adjusting its tension, then tie the other end on the opposite groove. Your bow is complete.

5 Arrows. A good-sized arrow should be about 2 feet (60 cm) long. Strip the bark off your straight branches and then whittle down any nubs for a smooth shaft.

6 Make a point. You've got two options: you can either sharpen the end for your arrow, or you can create an arrowhead. If you go the sharpened-stick method, temper the end in the fire to harden it. Good arrowhead options include sharp, flat stones, glass, and bone. Make a notch in the end of your arrow, slide your arrowhead in, and tie it into place tightly with your string.

7 Tie a few feathers to the blunt end of your arrow to help your arrow's accuracy during flight.

8 Lastly, notch a groove in the end with the feathers at a width that accommodates the bowstring comfortably. Take aim and fire away.

Tracking

Out in the woods, your senses will blossom, which is not to say that you walk around in a daze in your everyday city life, but that after a little while in the wilderness you'll hear with a new set of ears and see with a new set of eyes. Honing these sensations is the key to tracking. Be aware of everything around you, as clues about the animal you're after will come in various forms.

Think of tracking as reading, but instead of a book, you've got the forest floor to interpret. The "signs," as professional trackers refer to them, you see around you are written by the animal you're after.

SIGNS TO LOOK FOR

★ **Footprints**—A fresh paw print, indicating the animal is near, is usually well defined in its form. A weathered look, with cracked edges or no clear edge, means it's an old print.

★ **Fecal droppings**—Heat or a strong odor is an indication the animal may be near.

★ **Vegetation**—Look for flattened grassy areas or broken twigs. Trampled grass usually rises after a few hours, so if it's still flat you may be hot on the animal's trail. If broken twigs are green and new, they may be a clue that your animal has passed by recently.

★ **Fur or hair**—When seen on low-lying bushes, this is evidence that your animal has passed that way.

How to make a simple snare

Snares are simple traps that use a noose to catch the animal you're hunting but usually won't kill it. That's up to you. There are various types you can employ, but let's stick to a tried-and-true one that is fairly simple to set up.

YOU WILL NEED

✓ Rope or wire

✓ Two forked branches

✓ A tree or tree stump

STEPS

1 Make a noose big enough for your prey in the end of your wire. This will tighten around the animal's neck as it passes through it.

2 The two forked branches will hold your snare aloft, so consider what you're hunting, decide how far above the ground the snare should be, and then work the branches into the ground accordingly.

3 Anchor the wire end opposite the noose by tying it to a tree or tree stump.

4 Place the noose into the forks of the branches and then go hide.

TIP: This snare works best when set over a trail you're sure an animal travels, or when placed in front of their burrow. It rarely kills the animal, so be sure to check it often so you don't lose your catch to another wily predator. Also try to handle the snare as little as possible so you don't leave a heavy scent for the animal to pick up.

Deadfall traps

Traps can range from holes in the earth covered with large leaves to those that employ weight-and-trigger mechanisms. When in doubt as to design, just think about the simple variations you saw in episodes of the Road Runner cartoon as a kid. Oddly enough, Wile E. Coyote's techniques can sometimes work in the wild.

STEPS

You will need to find a heavy log or a large rock, some sturdy branches, your knife, and some good bait in order to construct your deadfall trap.

1 Make a trigger mechanism to fire the trap by sharpening both ends of a small, sturdy branch. Don't fully strip the branch; leave a small branch sticking out of this trigger so you can stick the bait on its end.

2 Sharpen the end of another sturdy branch, leaving the top end blunt, and then dig the sharp end into the ground. Make sure this branch is as tall as your trigger, as they'll both form the uprights to the trap.

3 Make the crossbar. This branch will span the trigger and the branch you've just put in the ground. Four feet (1.2 m) across is a good length for the crossbar branch. Leave one end as is, and whittle the other end at a 45-degree angle, creating a platform for the trigger stick's point to lock in place. Choose this branch wisely, as it needs to be strong enough to handle the weight of the logs or rock that will lie on top of it.

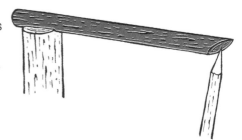

TIP: Bait placement is key. Make sure to position it well on the jutting branch, as this trap works best when the animal has to really work for it and pull hard on the bait, causing the trigger stick to collapse, or "fire," quickly on them.

4 Now place your bait on the trigger's small jutting branch, making sure to aim the bait toward the angle where the heavy logs will touch the ground. This will lure your prey further inside the trap.

5 Set the "as is" end of the crossbar on top of the sturdy upright branch with the 45-degree-angled end on the trigger branch. If you are having trouble, notch a small groove into the crossbar to ensure its adherence. The crossbar should be level when it spans. Balance the trigger on a slight angle to ensure it falls.

6 Carefully lay a heavy log on top of the crossbar to test the weight and sturdiness. Repeat with other logs. Carefully adjust the trigger and bait if needed.

TIP: Don't risk getting caught in this kind of trap by making it from the inside out. Work from the outside in.

A little trial and error is necessary with this one, as calibrating the trigger can be tricky, but stick with it and you'll be justly rewarded. The hardest part here will be lifting the heavy logs or large rock you intend to use to inflict the crushing blow.

Transporting and preparing your kill

Plucked dead from your trap, you can't eat a freshly caught rabbit like you'd eat an apple. Well, you could, but you'd get a mouthful of fur and have a pretty good chance of getting sick.

Bleeding and gutting your kill

Usually hunters bleed their kill first, which basically extracts the blood from the meat. If you want to attempt this step, tie the creature's hind legs from a wooden crossbar frame or tree branch, and let it hang as you slit its throat.

Gutting can be done as your prey hangs, or you can do it on the forest floor. Taking your knife in hand, start at the anus and run a careful cut—mind the guts to avoid a mess—up to the chest cavity past the breastbone. Remove the entrails, which should pull away rather easily.

Transporting your kill

Depending on the size of your catch and the distance you are from camp, you may run across some issues in hauling your goods. If you've got medium-sized animals like rabbits, you can just wrap them in your sack and head back to camp, or tie some rope around their legs and throw them over your shoulder.

As far as big game goes, it's easiest to just do as the caveman once did and drag it behind you. You can improvise a type of sled called a "travois" fairly easily by just lashing some medium-sized sticks in between two longer sticks that you'll then strap your kill to. This ends up resembling a long ladder that you drag behind you, taking the majority of the weight off of your actual body.

If there are two of you out there in the wilderness, you can tie the animal to a sturdy branch and span its weight between the two of you as you walk, hefting opposite ends of the branch on your shoulders with the kill suspended in the middle.

Skinning a rabbit

With a rabbit gutted and dangling before you, skinning it is the last step you need to take before you cook it.

STEPS

1 First, cut in a circle around the rabbit's hind legs with your knife.

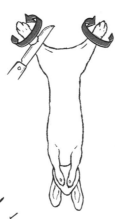

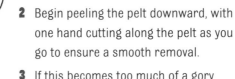

2 Begin peeling the pelt downward, with one hand cutting along the pelt as you go to ensure a smooth removal.

3 If this becomes too much of a gory scene for you, just try to imagine that the rabbit is hot and you're helping it take off its sweatshirt.

4 As you approach the neck, you can cut off the front legs and then just draw the pelt over its head.

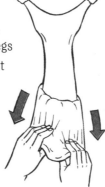

Smoking

A favorite among the mountain-man set, building a simple teepee smoker will allow you to preserve both meats and vegetables and lock in tons of flavor to boot.

YOU WILL NEED

- ✓ Three long sticks
- ✓ Twine
- ✓ Many small sticks
- ✓ Large leaves
- ✓ Fire
- ✓ Green leaves/wood

STEPS

1 Lash together the ends of all three long sticks with some twine, and then spread them out from the top to form a teepee triangle bound at the top.

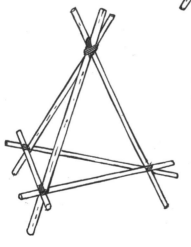

2 Taking three smaller sticks, span the gaps horizontally between the legs of your teepee about a foot (30 cm) up from the ground, and attach them with twine.

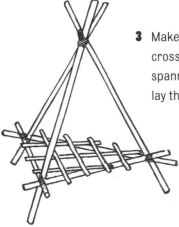

3 Make a grill using small sticks crosshatched across the horizontally spanning sticks. This is where you'll lay the meat to be smoked.

4 Light a fire and let it burn down to white-hot embers. Place the teepee smoker on top of it, and place the meat on the grill.

5 Now place some green leaves or greenwood on top of the embers to create the smoke that will flavor and preserve your meat.

TIP: If you want to speed the process up, you can drape the teepee smoker in larger leaves to keep more smoke inside. Just be careful to not let the fire go out.

Preserving and storing food

Cobbling together a refrigerator from natural means to keep your meat and fish fresh is an unlikely prospect without electricity. For the long-haul stay in the wilderness you'll want to preserve and immediately make last whatever it is you've caught. Realistically, you should always be preserving food, as you never know when food sources might suddenly get scarce.

Drying

Meat and fish can be dried outside if the correct temperatures are present; obviously it needs to be reasonably warm. This method can take a few days and works best if you can keep the meat in strong direct sunlight for the duration of those days. Setting up a simple ladderlike drying rack can allow you to dry many pieces of fish or meat at one time.

NATURAL PRESERVATIVES

★ **Salt**—This is an ancient tool for preserving fish. Rubbed into fish, it removes the water inside and stops the spoiling process. When salted well, particularly if salted in cold weather when the fish doesn't have time to spoil while drying, fish can keep for a year. Salting can also be used to preserve meat.

★ **Brine**—Saltwater can be used to pickle vegetables, too. Vegetables will last longer if they can then be suspended in an acidic solution such as vinegar.

★ **Lemons and limes**—The natural citric acid of these fruits is great for pickling fish or vegetables.

★ **Spices**—Various spices (fennel seed, mustard seed, cayenne pepper), when mixed in boiling water, will work wonders at pickling vegetables.

Long term: building a brick oven

You may never get tired of an open fire, but smoked meat and skewer-cooked fish might start to get old after a while. An outdoor brick oven isn't too easy to build, but it's easy to cook in and makes for a bigger menu at your log cabin.

YOU WILL NEED

✓ Cement

✓ Four 6-foot (1.8-m) long planks

✓ Bricks and mortar

✓ Concrete or metal lintel, 2 feet (60 cm) long

✓ Hardwood offcut, about a foot (30 cm) square

✓ 10–12 flexible branches or lengths of plywood about 5 feet (1.5 m) long

STEPS

1 First you need a base to keep your oven away from the damp and reduce fire risk. Build a square framework 6 feet (1.8 m) to a side out of your planks and find a flat area to lay it on.

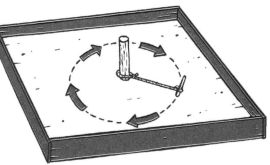

Fill it with cement to a depth of about 3 inches (8 cm). While the cement's still soft, put a small stake in the middle with an 18-inch (50-cm) string tied to it, and mark out a 3-foot (1-m) diameter circle for the outline of your oven.

2 When your base is dry, spread a layer of mortar around the circle and start building the walls. Lay the bricks in circular courses, remembering to leave a gap for the door. Leave each course to dry before laying the next one so your oven doesn't collapse. The mortar between the bricks needs to be thicker on the outside of the circle than on the inside, to keep the circle true. Build walls up to a height of about 18 inches (50 cm).

3 The bigger the doorway, the bigger the items you can cook. The smaller the doorway, the longer your oven will stay hot. A foot (30 cm) square is a good compromise. Leave a gap of the right size in your wall and close it with a lintel built into the top course of bricks. Preferably use a concrete lintel, because it conducts less heat than metal and so will keep your oven hotter. Wood is not so good—if it burns through, there's a good chance your oven will collapse.

4 The door won't be in place while the oven is burning, so you can make it out of a thick piece of hardwood. Cut it roughly to size with an ax, then trim it with a knife or chisel so it can be wedged over the doorway to keep the heat in while cooking.

5 Now comes the tricky part: building the dome. You'll need a frame to support your bricks while the mortar hardens. When your walls are set, take 10–12 flexible lengths of wood and fit the ends inside the oven walls so they arch over the top and outline your dome. Then lay the bricks in courses following this shape, with the mortar thicker on the outside as with the walls, but tilting the bricks in as well as around. You'll need less bricks for each circle as your dome gets higher. Do the last few rows in a spiral pattern to close the circle. You may need to split the bricks with a chisel as you get near the top of the dome and the courses start to get tight. Top off with half a brick surrounded by mortar to close any last gaps.

6 Sit back and admire your bricklaying while the mortar dries. When it's set, spread a thin layer of cement over everything for insulation and weather-proofing, and to give it a good finish. Remember to take the wooden supports out of the dome before you start cooking, unless you like your stew flavored with charcoal! Lay heatproof tiles or firebricks on the floor inside to cook on, and you're ready to go.

7 You may now be looking at the inside of your oven and wondering how you're going to fit a fire and a cookpot inside. The good news is you don't have to. The brick oven works by heating the bricks with a fire, then raking out the fire and using the hot bricks to cook your dinner. Your first fire should be a small one and only burn for about an hour. This makes sure the mortar is properly dried out.

8 When you're ready to cook, build a small teepee fire in the center of the oven and keep it burning for about an hour. Leave the door off, because the ventilation will make the fire burn hotter. When the inside of the oven is good and hot, rake out the cinders and ash (making sure to put them where they won't set fire to anything else), and put your dinner inside. Fish wrapped in foil cooks well, so does pizza or a pot of rabbit stew. Put the door on to keep the heat in, and leave it to bake.

TIP: Some ovens take longer to heat up than others, and some stay hotter for longer. You can experiment with different heating/cooking times, or use a thermometer to figure out the best timing.

CHAPTER 6

On the move

Which way do you run when you wake in the morning and realize that the pitter-patter of rain that lulled you to sleep the night before turned into a deluge while you slumbered away, and now floodwaters are inching ever higher toward your site?

Or what about when you're numb with sheer boredom with your surroundings, like being sick of all those stupid whistling pine trees crowding out your view of the mountaintop? Will you be able to tell east from west when you strike camp and set out for a better view?

Whatever the impetus, moving through nature takes a combination of some basic skills and some good old common sense. Let's get a move on!

Compass and map basics

If by navigation you mean figuring out how to get to happy hour in as few subway stops as possible on a Friday night, the thought of mastering how to get from point A to point B in the wilderness may seem to have a steep learning curve.

Luckily, the two things to know here are basic geography and basic science. Firstly, the earth is divided into two hemispheres, north and south, by the equator, and no matter which hemisphere your feet are in, the sun rises in the east and sets in the west—always. So if the sun's out, you have a good chance of orienting yourself properly. As for science, this ever-spinning Earth of ours has a magnetic core, and out of its ends (poles) comes a charge, and if you have a magnetic compass with you, you'll be able to calculate directions exactly. Finding your way in the wilderness, like life, is just a matter of knowing exactly where it is you are and then finding exactly where it is you want to go. With a compass and map on hand you're well on your way.

A compass will pick up the magnetic charges mentioned above and then indicate what's known as magnetic north, which is not to be confused with the true north (or grid north) that maps are set to. This difference shouldn't scare you: the variation between these two norths is slight in most parts of the world. Most maps will include the exact magnetic variation (sometimes referred to as "declination") of the area, so that if necessary you can adjust your compass properly.

Maps can vary in scope and scale, but even the most basic will give you both vertical and horizontal lines and come with a legend or key that helps explain how that particular map works. Before you set off, be sure to take note of your natural surroundings and try to match up what you see on the ground with what you see on your map.

Your compass and map will function independently of one another, but fused together they realize their full potential as the key tools of navigation, helping you find which way you're headed as you roam around in the wild.

Combining compass and map

ORIENTING YOUR MAP WITH THE AID OF YOUR COMPASS

1 Place your map on level ground and put the compass on it, aligning it with the right or left margin, let the compass needle find magnetic north.

2 Keeping the compass stationary, rotate the map until its vertical lines (indicating true north) match up with the compass needle (indicating magnetic north). The map is now set to the world around you and can be read properly.

GETTING FROM A TO B WITH MAP AND COMPASS

1 Pick out a destination in the distance, like that plateau over yonder.

2 Place your compass on the map, forming a straight line with your baseplate's edge between where you are now (A) and your destination (B). When done correctly, the direction arrow at the top of your baseplate will also point in the direction of B.

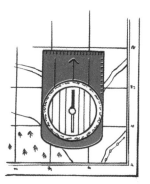

TIP: Check the distance between points A and B by reading the measurements on your baseplate's edge and comparing it to the map's actual scale.

3 Without moving the compass, rotate the bezel—that central dial in the middle—until its north arrow aligns itself with the north–south lines on your map. This sets your bearing into the compass.

4 Slowly turn the map until the north arrow on the dial lines up with the compass's magnetic north needle. The direction arrow at the top of your baseplate will point out your bearing. You can now walk with the compass in hand, and as long as the needle is aligned with the north arrow on the bezel, the arrow on the baseplate will point in the direction you want to go. Make sure as you walk toward that plateau that you hold the compass level horizontally.

How to improvise a compass

YOU WILL NEED

✓ A piece of ferrous metal—a sewing needle, a paper clip, or nail

✓ A magnet, or a piece of synthetic material like fleece or silk

✓ A bowl or cup

✓ Water

✓ A leaf or blade of grass

STEPS

1 Start by running the magnet over the needle, always in the same direction, about ten times. This magnetizes the needle. Those without a magnet will need to stroke the needle with their swatch of synthetic material much more than ten times—try 50—always in the same direction. It's a static electric charge you're going for here, so the more you stroke the stronger the charge will be. Mind the pointed end.

2 Fill your bowl or cup with water.

3 Float your leaf or blade of grass on the surface of the water.

4 Place the magnetized needle on the leaf and watch as it magically aligns itself north–south.

Finding your way without a compass

You're a few miles in on a hike when you realize you've veered off the track a bit. After a frantic search of your pack, you come to the harsh realization that you've left your compass back at home. Believe it or not, you've still got a few options left.

Do you have the time?

If you're wearing a watch and it has hands on it, you've probably been called "old school" by someone half your age, but what's even more old school is to turn that timepiece into a makeshift compass.

If you're in the northern hemisphere, hold your watch in a horizontal position and point the hour hand directly at the sun. Keeping it still, just imagine a line bisecting between the hour hand and the 12 o'clock mark on your watch. This creates an instant north–south line, with the southerly direction indicated by the top of this imaginary line.

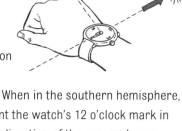

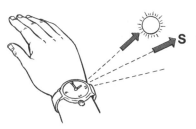

When in the southern hemisphere, point the watch's 12 o'clock mark in the direction of the sun, and your north–south line will be the bisection between this and wherever the hour hand is, with the top of this line giving you a rough indication of north.

> **TIP:** If you're a bit "new school," and you only have a digital watch, just note the time on your watch and then draw out an old-school watch— either on paper with a pencil or just right there in the dirt with a stick— and apply the above principles.

Shadow sticks

Another method for finding your way is by reading shadows. It's pretty basic, and depending on your time crunch, it can be executed in about 15 minutes.

STEPS

All you will need to orient yourself reading shadows is a stick and two stones.

1 Find a straight stick about 3 feet (1 m) long.

2 Plant it in level ground so it stands up straight, where it can cast back a clear shadow.

3 Mark the tip of this initial shadow with one of your two stones. This will be your "west" mark anywhere on earth.

4 Wait at least 15 minutes, then go back and check the shadow's progress, as it will have moved.

5 Mark the new shadow tip with your other stone, and you will have an "east" mark.

6 By drawing a line between the two marks, you make an east–west line, with north and south at right angles to this line. Place your left foot on the east mark and your right foot on the west mark, and you'll be facing north.

Natural indicators of direction

Plants, no matter the locale, need the sun in order to grow, so they grow toward its direction. In the northern hemisphere, plants and trees will be more dense, or lush in appearance, on their south-facing side, and flowers will likewise bloom in the sun's direct line. Flip this around for southern hemisphere flora.

TIP: If you should come across any tree stumps, you can also decipher the growth rings to determine direction, as they'll be more plentiful on the equator side.

Navigating by the stars

When forced to travel at night, you'll need to consult the stars as an indicator of direction. Peering into the night sky can be an intimidating prospect, but just do as many generations of seafaring people have done before you and put your trust in the stars.

Just like in the previous examples with the watch compass and our shadow stick, your choice of stars depends on whether you are in the northern or southern hemisphere. In the northern hemisphere, the star you need to find is appropriately called the North Star and just happens to be one of the brightest. In order to find it, first seek out that soup ladle to the gods, the constellation known as the Big Dipper. Then make an imaginary line using the two stars that form the Big Dipper's front lip, continue this line out of the ladle about five times its original length. You should arrive at the North Star. Now just draw an

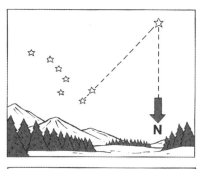

imaginary line from the North Star, which sits directly over the North Pole, on down to Earth, and you've got your northerly direction.

Unfortunately, in the southern hemisphere there's no bright South Star pointing the way. In its place, there's a constellation known as the Southern Cross. Once you've picked out the four bright stars that form the cross, look to the two stars that make the longer of the two crossbeams, and these will point your way. Now just extend this crossbeam out about five times and mark that imaginary point in the sky. A line carried from that point in the sky and then brought down to Earth will give you an approximate southerly direction.

Signaling for help

Your smartphone won't get reception out here, so there won't be any 911 calls or texting of SOSs to loved ones. And shame on you if you actually brought the darn thing out here with you—after all, wasn't the whole point of the trip to get away from the grind of daily life?

What you need to do first is get out of the thickets of the trees and find some wide-open area where you can create a proper signal for help. If you've got the raw material around, you can start a fire. The smokier the fire, the better chance you have of attracting a rescue party. Make sure to amass a good amount of greenwood: any fresh leaves, boughs, or moss will do the trick. Anything damp will give off a steady white plume of smoke once thrown on an already burning fire, and this should help get you spotted.

Also, dig around in your pack for a mirror (sometimes included in first-aid kits) or any kind of polished metal, like lids from your camp cookware, or even that CD of campfire songs your roommate burned for you that only made it into your pack because you didn't want to hurt her feelings; these items can all help you send a distress signal. Take one of these reflective items and hold it out in front of you. What you're doing is capturing the sun's light in your reflector so you can then beam this light, by subtly moving the reflector, in any direction to signal for help. Used correctly, these reflections can be seen at a distance of up to 50 miles (80 km). Now just wait for a passing rescue helicopter and show them the light.

If you're having trouble lining up your reflected light with your target, start by aiming at the ground in front of you. Get the reflected spot pointing in the right direction first, then raise the elevation to the appropriate angle.

Morse code

This is an invaluable-to-learn alphabet of blips and hyphens that could one day save your life. Speaking Morse can be done with all different things—from a flashlight or reflector to a radio, or even whistled if you've got the pipes. Just remember the blips are short and the dashes are long. Save Our Souls (SOS) is the international distress signal, so if you can't get all these committed to memory, at least remember that one and you'll be okay.

```
SOS . . . _ _ _ . . .

A . _    B _ . . .   C _ . _ .  D _ . .   E .      F . . _ .  G _ _ .   H . . . .
I . .     J . _ _ _  K _ . _    L . _ . .  M _ _    N _ .      O _ _ _   P . _ _ .
Q _ _ . _ R . _ .   S . . .    T _       U . . _   V . . . _  W . _ _   X _ . . _
Y _ . _ _ Z _ _ . .
```

International ground-to-air code

Another method of signaling, this one involves a little bit more physical work than the others. Felled trees or rocks work well, or you can even attempt the crop-circle method and just push down the natural vegetation that surrounds you. Make sure to exaggerate everything. You're going for size here—remember that it needs to be visible from the air.

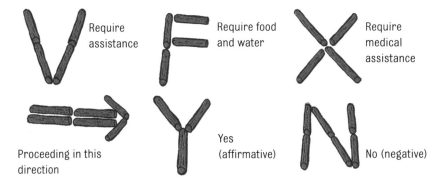

Require assistance

Require food and water

Require medical assistance

Proceeding in this direction

Yes (affirmative)

No (negative)

Building a canoe and paddle

Time is your biggest obstacle when it comes to crafting a canoe from scratch. Not only does it take quite a while to shape the thing, it also takes a couple of patient months as you wait for your newly felled tree to dry out.

STEPS

1 Pick a tree of appropriate size for your canoe purposes. Chop away. Once felled, cut off all the branches. Leave the felled tree to dry out for a few months.

2 With your ax and knife, begin to shape the outside first. A basic rough shape will do fine to start with. Think of your log, as viewed from bow to stern (front to back), coming to look like a cross between the letters U and V.

3 Once you have the outside hull shaped, you can move inward to create your seating area. To speed the process up, make a fire and then collect some of its white-hot embers. Place the embers on the top of your canoe and let them burn/smoke down through the wood a few inches. Remove them and then scrape away the ash with your ax blade. Repeat many times.

4 Fashion a paddle out of sturdy tree branches, preferably still green. Choose a thick branch about 6 feet (1.8 m) long. With your knife, square the bottom 1 foot (30 cm) of one end of the branch, creating a kind of long rectangle. Now with two smaller branches, each about a foot (30 cm) long, shape their entire lengths into matching rectangles with your knife. Then sandwich the rectangled part of the long branch in between the two shorter ones and bind it all together with twine.

5 Give the canoe a test-float in shallow water and check for leaks. Tree sap works well for plugging the holes in your canoe.

6 Bust out that travel-sized bottle of Veuve Clicquot, christen her, and you're on your way upriver. Paddle on.

Making an emergency raft

So you've just spent the last few hours wading in and out of a river, carefully selecting rocks for an epic fire pit, and now it's time to transport them. The path you took to get here was far too arduous even with just the weight of your backpack to contend with. How are you going to get all those heavy stones back to camp? You step back and take in the river for a moment when you notice a twig merrily floating by. A second passes, and the synapses connect. "That's it," you think, "a raft. I'll build a raft and float these rocks downstream to camp."

YOU WILL NEED

- ✓ A knife
- ✓ A wire saw
- ✓ Rope
- ✓ Logs

> **TIP:** When building a raft, just think of making a sandwich. The same building elements are present—just the essentials: bread and meat.

STEPS

1 Find some downed trees. If you can't locate any, seek out some mid-size younger trees that you can cut down with a wire saw without too much trouble.

> **TIP:** Wire saws often come in survival kits. They take up much less space than bladed saws but are only good for cutting smaller logs. Loop rope or cloth through the wire handles so you don't cut your hands when you use it.

2 Start sawing away. Cut enough logs at the desired length to give you a wide enough base for your load. The size of the raft can be anywhere from 6 x 6 feet (2 x 2 m) to 12 x 12 feet (4 x 4 m)—you be the judge. Bring all your logs close to the water for the building process; it's easier to launch this sucker if you don't have to drag it a couple hundred feet to the river first.

3 On four logs (the bread), you need to saw out, or notch out, some wood along their length. Don't go too deep—a few inches should do.

4 Lay out two of these notched logs parallel to each other and then complete a square with two other logs that have not been notched out, overlapping them at the right-angle corners to form Vs with the protruding ends.

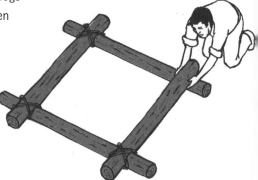

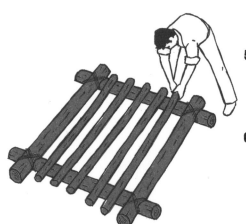

5 Then go ahead and secure those corners really well with rope and some basic sturdy knots.

6 Now build the deck (the meat). Lay a few logs to span across the two notched-out logs from step 4. Repeat with all logs until the deck is finished.

TIP: Invariably, some logs will be heavier than others. Distribute them so that you don't weigh your raft down in any one spot.

7 Lay your other two leftover notched-out logs (leftover bread) from step 3 on top of the logs that form your deck, sandwiching the deck between them, and you're ready to cap your raft.

8 Tie up all four corners with rope like you did in step 5, making sure to lash the outsides of the bread together, squeezing the meat taut between the bread so that no meat gets out once the bread gets wet. Do the same to the middle section of the raft, and you're now ready to launch the vessel. Enjoy the ride.

Navigating your vessel

For steering purposes, you can either use a long, sturdy branch to push yourself along or create a basic rudder to attach to the back of your raft. For the rudder, just mimic the steps for building a canoe paddle (see page 134) and then lash it to your raft.

Conclusion

The practice sessions are long behind you. You can't mold any more mock snow caves out of your sofa and your 600 fill-count goose-down comforter, and the neighbors have finally wised up to your nighttime foraging in their herb garden. So, after purchasing all the necessary gear, reading and rereading the maps a few times, and having somehow managed to get time off work, you're finally ready for your wilderness adventure to begin. It's now time for Mother Nature and all her glory.

No need to worry, you can do this. Sure, before you're up there on the top of the mountain there's a lot of work to be done in preparation, and sometimes your execution of a new skill may lead you to curse a blue streak, but step back for just a moment. Take a nice deep breath. When that pure mountain air fills your lungs, turn and check out the view of the surrounding gorge and that crystalline blue lake off in the distance. Exhale, then try getting that fire going from scratch again. The sense of accomplishment you'll get from seeing those sparks turn to flames using only the barest of necessities will be like nothing you've ever experienced.

With all of that said, once away from the rat race of city life, make sure you're completely open to the wondrous ways of the wild—it has many lessons to teach. And don't go forgetting the most important thing while in the great outdoors, which is to simply enjoy yourself. So go ahead, savor a night sleeping under the stars, watching the wisps of smoke from your fire dance up through the treetops to a soundtrack of pining crickets and the nearby rushing river. Or delight in waking with the sun and taking an invigorating morning hike before you hit the river to catch your brunch of wild rainbow trout. It's all out there waiting for you, so get going. No matter the destination—be it mountain, desert, or jungle—know that a life in the wild, or even just a three-day weekend, can be an exhilarating, empowering, and, more often than not, truly life-changing experience.

Appendix: first aid

There's no easy way around it, accidents on the trail can befall you at any moment, whether you're a novice hiker or a seasoned backpacker. So, should you slip while gutting a fish and cut your hand, burn yourself lighting a fire, twist an ankle on a switchback, or suffer an arm fracture falling out of a tree while collecting fruit, here are some tried and true methods to patch yourself up and get back on the trail.

Lacerations

Clean the cut. Run cold water over it as soon as possible. If you have antiseptic spray or gel in your kit, use it now. With a piece of gauze, a shirt, or any fabric, apply pressure to the cut, keeping it closed, to stop the flow of blood. Try to elevate the cut area above the heart to help stem bloodflow. Secure the closure by spanning the wound with a butterfly bandage. Adhere one side of the bandage to one side of the wound. With the other side of the bandage, pull the cut closed and adhere the bandage. Repeat this over the length of the laceration to ensure proper closure. Dress the wound firmly with gauze, making sure not to bind too tight or too loose.

Burns

As soon as possible, run cool water over the burn to lessen the pain. Do not use ice, which can actually damage your skin more. When the pain has subsided enough, gently wash the burn with soap and warm water to remove any dirt or ashes from the wound. Gently pat dry the burn. Wrap the injured area of skin with dry gauze to keep it clean and protected. If the pain persists, try taking an over-the-counter painkiller like aspirin, ibuprofen, or acetaminophen. Wash the wound with soap and water, and replace the gauze dressing every day. If the old dressing sticks to the burn you might have to soak it off with water.

Sprains

For sprains, follow the acronym R.I.C.E., and with time the sprain will eventually heal itself.

R.I.C.E. = REST, ICE, COMPRESSION, AND ELEVATION

★ **R**—First try and find a spot to rest and assess your situation.

★ **I**—If you have ice, apply it immediately to the area to reduce the swelling. If you're without ice, submerge the injury in a cold stream.

★ **C**—Firmly wrap an elastic or gauzelike bandage around the joint to immobilize the area. If you absolutely have to keep walking on a sprained ankle, lace your boot tight and use it as a brace for the injury.

★ **E**—Elevate the limb to prevent further swelling.

Broken bones

The fracture of a bone will be jarring and quite painful, and more often than not you can tell when it's happened. First things first: you need to assess exactly where the break is. Try to move the area as little as possible as you examine it. Once the break is identified, it's time to splint the limb. Splints can take many shapes and sizes, but just make sure they're rigid enough to keep a broken bone aligned. Branches, ax handles, even a ski pole will work. Cushion the injured limb with some padding (a shirt or something), then sandwich the injured limb between two splints and tie them—not too tight—above and below the break.

TIP: A broken bone is a serious injury, so don't attempt to treat it yourself unless you have absolutely no other options. It's a much better idea to call in the paramedics and get the professionals to patch you up.

Index